The Standard Deviants

STUDY SIDEKICK

The Stimulating World of Psychology
Study Sidekick - 1st Edition

Written by The Standard Deviants® Academic Team, including:
Lisa Fishman, Doctoral Candidate, Psychology
Celia Lescano, Doctoral Candidate, Psychology
Igor Torgeson

Edited by:
Jennie Halfant

Contributing Editors:
Katherine Ross-Kidder, Ph.D.
Igor Torgeson
Celia Lescano, Doctoral Candidate, Psychology
Chip Paucek

Graphic Design by:
Joe Braband

Cover Design by:
C. Christopher Stevens

800-238-9669
e-mail: cerebellum@mindspring.com
www.cerebellum.com

STUDY SIDEKICK

Other subjects from Cerebellum:

Finance

Accounting

Microeconomics

Statistics

Calculus 1 & 2

Pre-Calculus 1 & 2

Algebra 1 & 2

Biology

Physics

Chemistry 1, 2, & 3

Basic Math

Trigonometry

Geology

Printed in the beautiful U.S.A.

HOW TO USE THIS BOOK

→ **WATCH THE VIDEO.** This STANDARD DEVIANTS STUDY SIDEKICK will help you much more if you use it in conjunction with "The Stimulating World of Psychology."

→ **FOLLOW ALONG.** The **VIDEO NOTES** section does your work for you! We've already taken all of your notes--all you have to do is follow along with the video.

We've even given you a **VIDEO TIME CODE**. Just reset your VCR counter to 0:00:00 on the Cerebellum logo. These clocks 0:00:00 give you the time code for each important section so you know where to fast forward to! This will enable you to learn and retain material much more effectively. Just pause the tape after a difficult section and read through your notes!

→ **LEARN NEW STUFF.** Unfortunately, we just can't get to everything in the video. The **OTHER IMPORTANT STUFF** section gives any other cool facts you'll need to ace your tests.

→ **TEST YOURSELF.** **QUIZZES** and **PRACTICE EXAMS** allow you to test yourself and make sure you've covered all the bases. The answers appear at the back--*don't cheat!*

→ **HAVE FUN.** The book is chock-full of diversions and stress-relievers, and there's two of those neat flippy pictures on the bottom of the pages.

STUDY SIDEKICK

TABLE OF CONTENTS

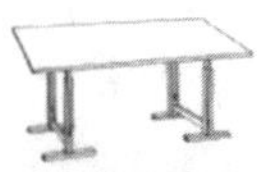

Table of Contents

STUDY SIDEKICK

VIDEO TIME CODE

0:14:04 .... 2. research designs

0:14:30 .... a. experimental studies

0:14:47 .... i. independent variables

0:14:53 .... ii. dependent variables

0:15:47 .... iii. operational definitions

0:19:20 .... b. correlational studies

0:20:05 .... i. positive correlations

0:20:36 .... ii. negative correlations

0:21:50 .... c. descriptive studies

0:23:21 .... C. Neurons and the Nervous System

0:28:00 .... D. Sensation

0:31:57 .... E. Motivation

0:37:03 .... F: Emotion

0:39:42 **II. Learning and Cognition**

0:41:33 .... A. Classical Conditioning

0:52:50 .... B. Operant Conditioning

1:00:14 .... C. Social Learning

1:01:34 .... D. Memory and Forgetting

1:08:33 .... E. Cognitive Development and Jean Piaget

Video Time Code

VIDEO NOTES

0:02:35

Part I: Introduction--Get Psyched!

Psychology is the study of behaviors and mental processes. *Behaviors* are what you can see a person do or the observable actions of an individual. *Mental processes* are cool things like memories, thoughts, dreams, emotional feelings, and other conscious or unconscious experiences.

Psychology is a science that attempts to describe, understand, and predict human behaviors and mental processes. Psychologists observe behaviors, then try to predict, control or modify future behaviors based on what they've seen.

Section A: Psychological Schools of Thought and the Nature-Nurture Debate

0:04:25

Psychology studies behaviors and mental processes. This suggests that behaviors and mental processes must vary across individuals. The study of the differences among individuals spurs the age-old **nature-nurture debate**: 0:05:26

> "Are people born to act and think the way they do, or is behavior determined by the environment?"

When a rambunctious kid is bouncing off the walls, the teacher asks:

> "Does Billy misbehave because he inherited the tendency to be very active, or does he misbehave because of the way his parents raise him?"

- The **nature** viewpoint: Billy *inherited* the tendency to be active; biology determines the child's behavior
- The **nurture** viewpoint: Billy gets lots of attention from his parents when he misbehaves, so Billy

misbehaves because he *likes* the attention; Billy's *environment* determines his behavior

- Most psychologists believe both nature *and* nurture play significant roles in shaping human behavior
- The critical question: *how much* does nature or nurture determine behavior?

0:07:10

The are five different **Psychological Schools of Thought: Biological**, **Psychoanalytic**, **Behavioral**, **Cognitive**, and **Humanistic**. All the schools of thought try to describe, understand, predict, and control or modify behavior. How do each of the psychological schools of thought approach Billy's temper tantrums?

Video Notes

0:08:15

Biological:

- There isn't much to do about it
- Since behavior is inherited, Billy is born as a naughty little behavior problem

0:08:30

Psychoanalytic:

- Associated with *Sigmund Freud*
- Tries to understand Billy's behavior by looking at what unconscious thoughts and conflicts he might be having based on the psychosexual stage he's passing through

0:08:50

Behavioral:

- Associated with *B.F. Skinner*
- Accuses the mother of reinforcing his temper tantrums by rewarding him after each outburst

0:09:22

Cognitive:

- Associated with *Jean Piaget*
- Tries to understand Billy's behavior by looking at what conscious thought processes Billy might be having based on the cognitive stage of develop-

ment he's passing through

- Tries to understand his behavior by basing conclusions on the concepts of accommodation and assimilation

0:09:42

Humanistic:

- Associated with ***Carl Rogers***
- There's nothing wrong with Billy; he's just a good kid trying to figure out who he is and how to maximize his potential

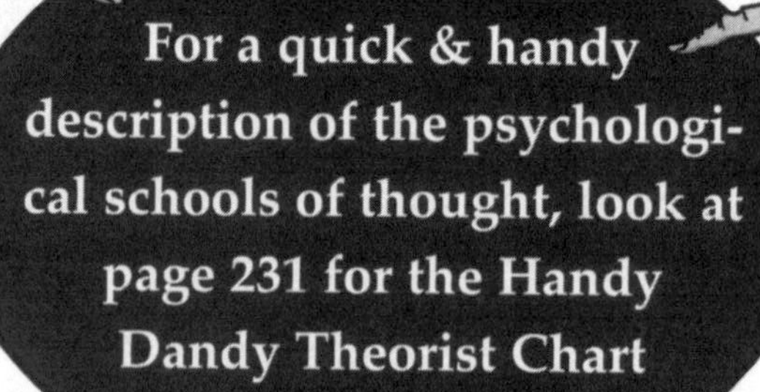

Video Notes

SUMMARY

- If behavior is controlled by genetics and biological functions, then behavior is controlled by **nature**
- If people learn how to act from their environment, then behavior is controlled by **nurture**
- In the **nature-nurture debate**, the most popular opinion is that behavior is controlled by both nature and nurture
- The real debate is how much nature controls and how much nurture controls
- The followers of all the major psychological schools of thought have the same goals: to describe, understand, predict, and control or modify behavior
- The Psychological Schools of Thought:
    - Biological
    - Psychoanalytic
    - Behavioral
    - Cognitive
    - Humanistic

0:11:00

Section B: Psychological Experiments

The Scientific Method:

Psychologists use the **scientific method** to study psychological phenomena. The scientific method is a process of developing theories or explanations of behavior. The scientific method is a four step process that goes something like this:

1) Develop a *theory*. ("My mom is lame.")

2) Form a *hypothesis:* a testable prediction implied by the theory. ("My mom is lame because she won't let me see my favorite band in concert.")

3) Conduct a *study* that suggests a cause and effect relationship. (Ask Mom, "Can I go see the Sound Butchers in concert tonight?")

4) After the study, take your results and adjust your original prediction. ("Mom may be pretty cool.")

Once you've conducted the study, design another study to test your *refined theory* and hypothesis.

Video Notes

0:11:33

Research Methods:

Psychologists use **research methods** to gather information. The three types of research methods are:

tests

interviews

observations

0:13:11

Tests look at how a subject responds to a particular event or problem. Tests must be *reliable* and *valid.*

- To be *reliable,* tests have to produce results that are consistent and predictable
- To be *valid,* tests must measure what they are designed to measure

0:13:27

Interviews study how the subject describes herself as she talks with the interviewer.

Observations are descriptions that the investigator makes of the subject. Observations can be made in either a *laboratory* setting or a *natural* setting, like someone's home or workplace.

0:13:47

- *Case studies* are more in-depth observations that investigators use to gather lots of information about different subjects

Psychologists use information collected through these various research methods to draw conclusions that they hope are applicable to a wide range of people.

0:14:04

Research Designs:

There are three basic **research designs**, or ways to set up an experiment:

experimental studies

correlational studies

descriptive studies

VIDEO NOTES

Psychologists use research designs to understand how one variable affects another.

The Experimental Study: 0:14:30

- Enables researchers to make the most solid conclusions regarding causation
- Investigator manipulates one or more factors in order to see what affect that factor has on behaviors or mental processes
    - **independent variable:** the experimental factor the investigator manipulates 0:14:47
    - **dependent variable:** the effect the investigator gets from the experiment; the effect *depends* on the independent variable 0:14:53

When researchers conduct an experiment and observe the results, they want to be certain that the factor they manipulated is the same factor that caused the results. So here's what they do:

- Researchers **randomly assign** their research subjects into two groups, the **experimental group** and the **control group**
- Both groups are exposed to the exact same con-

ditions, *but* the experimental group is also exposed to the manipulation of the independent variable

- All conditions are the same for the experimental group and the control group except for the thing the researcher is tinkering with
- **Random assignment:** used to assure that differences in the results between the two groups are not due to differences in the subjects
- All research studies should be **replicable**: other researchers should be able to repeat the experiment so the results can be further proved or disproved. Researchers should be able to repeat the same experiment and get the same results 95 out of 100 times.
- In order for a study to be repeated exactly the way it was done the first time, the researchers who design the study have to carefully describe the independent and dependent variables; they also have to write down a list (the **operational definitions**) of the exact procedures they followed to do the experiment.

0:15:47

Video Notes

The Correlational Study: 0:19:20

- Examines the *relationships* between the variables (the things they want to study)
- Researcher does not have control over the variables, but simply studies the relationship(s) between them
- Can look at the extent to which two factors vary together, but reliable assertions regarding whether change in one variable *causes* a change in the other cannot be made.

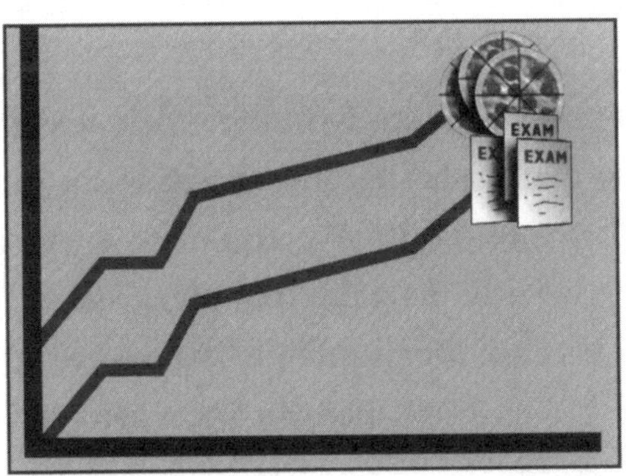

- **Positive correlation:** suggests a direct relationship between two variables; if one increases or decreases, so does the other 0:20:05

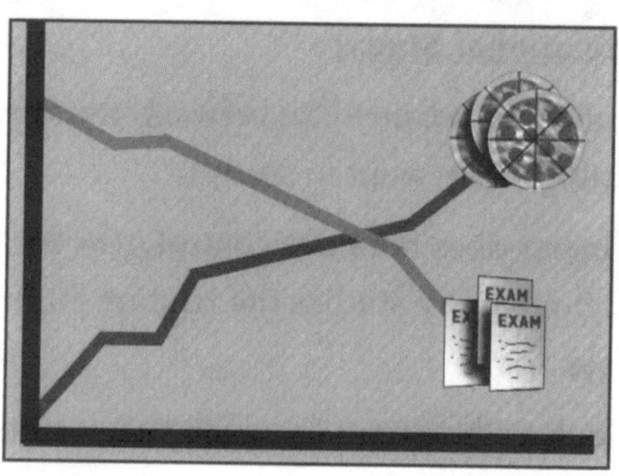

0:20:36

- **Negative correlation:** suggests an inverse relationship between two variables; if one increases, the other decreases, or vice versa

In the pizza sales study in the video, was there an increase in pizza sales because it was exam week or because it was cold out? We don't know. As a researcher, we *want* to claim that pizza sales increased because the number of exams being given increased; but as a scientist, we know we can only assert that increased pizza sales *seem to be related* to the number of exams given.

VIDEO NOTES

0:21:50

The Descriptive Study:

- Researchers find a systematic way to observe individuals and then describe their behaviors
- The investigators may use their descriptions to form a hypothesis
- After the investigator has formed a hypothesis, she may design an experiment to test the hypothesis

SUMMARY

- Psychologists do experiments using the scientific method
  - First they develop a theory
  - Next they form a hypothesis
  - Then they conduct a study
  - Finally, they adjust the hypothesis according to the results of the study and design another study to test the refined hypothesis
- There are three ways, or research designs, that psychologists use to set up an experiment:
  - experimental studies: researchers manipulate factors called independent variables to see what happens
  - correlational studies: look at relationships between variables
  - descriptive studies: researchers write down descriptions of what they observe and use these descriptions to help them form a hypothesis and set up a study

Section C: Neurons and the Nervous System

0:23:21

Your nervous system carries chemical and electrical signals from your body to your brain and from your brain to your body. Before we can understand our actions, memories, and feelings, we need to understand how information from the environment gets into our bodies and how our bodies process this information.

There are two components of the nervous system:

the central nervous system

the peripheral nervous system

- **Central nervous system (CNS):** consists of the brain and the spinal cord
- **Peripheral nervous system (PNS):** contains the neurons that connect the CNS to the rest of the body

Information is received by sense organs (like our eyes and ears) by way of *sense receptors*. These *sense receptors* change environmental energy into electronic energy, then send it down a highway of *sensory neurons* to the brain. Our different senses "talk" to our brain

through *sensory neurons*. *Motor neurons* carry messages in the opposite direction--*from* the CNS *to* the muscles and glands. *Interneurons* carry messages between neurons.

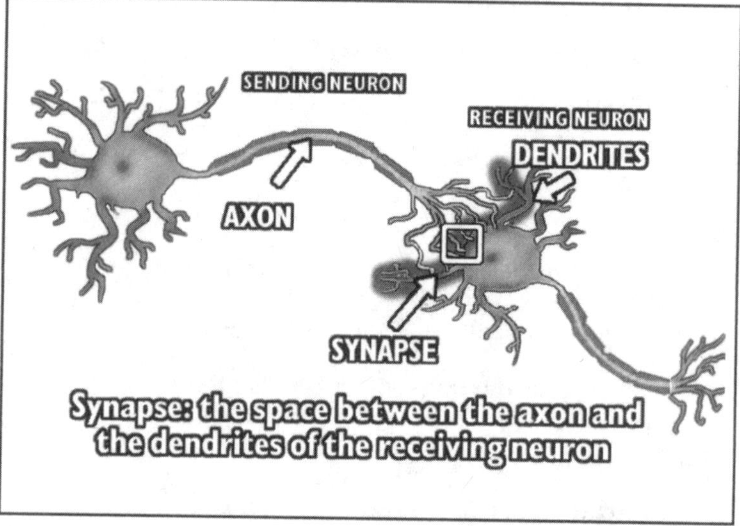

Neurons are the basic building blocks of the nervous system. They're made up of a bunch of little parts that work together to send electrical and chemical messages on their way from one part of the body to another, and from one neuron to another.

First, the **dendrites** receive the neural messages or impulses coming in from other neurons. The message is then sent to the **cell body** and on through the **axon**, an extension of the neuron which carries the message

through its branching fibers to the dendrites of the next neuron. The axon is insulated by a layer of fatty cells called the **myelin sheath**, which speeds up the travel of impulses.

To travel from one neuron to the next, a signal has to cross a **synapse**, the space between the axon of the sending neuron and the dendrites of the receiving neuron. The signal rides across this space, called the *synaptic gap*, on chemical messengers called **neurotransmitters**, which carry messages across the synaptic gap by attaching themselves to the receiving neuron. Dopamine and acetylcholine are examples of neurotransmitters. The neurotransmitter and the neuron must fit together like puzzle pieces--otherwise the neurotransmitter will not be taken up.

Neurons fire impulses when they are stimulated by some kind of electrical energy, like a stimulation from the environment or an impulse coming in from another neuron. The impulse is a quick electrical charge called an **action potential**. Neurons never fire half a shot; like guns, they either fire or they don't [it's an all or nothing thing with them--in fact, it's called "all or none" firing]. It's like turning a light on or off. None of this sissy dimmer switch stuff. It's all or nothing for neurons.

SUMMARY

- The nervous system is a way your body's parts communicate with each other
- The peripheral nervous system (PNS) sends signals from the body to the central nervous system (CNS)
- Sensory neurons carry electrical impulses through the peripheral nervous system to the brain, and motor neurons carry messages from the brain to the muscles and glands
- Interneurons carry messages between neurons
- Neurotransmitters, like dopamine and acetylcholine, are chemicals that carry the message across the synaptic gap between one neuron and the next
- As soon as neurons receive that message in the form of an electrical impulse called the action potential, neurons fire
- Neurons, like guns, either fire or they don't; this is called "all or none" firing

Section D: Sensation

0:28:00

Sensation is the way your sense receptors and nervous system take in information and turn it into the chemicals and electrical impulses that zoom through your body and brain with the information.

The **absolute threshold** of a stimulus is the smallest amount of a stimulus that you can detect; if you can just barely see a light, so that if it were any dimmer you couldn't see it at all, you'd be at the absolute threshold of the stimulus (the light).

The **difference threshold** is the smallest difference a person can detect between two stimuli. If you can just barely hear a difference between two notes, then you may be at the difference threshold for those notes. The difference threshold is also called the **just noticeable difference** or **jnd.**

JND

Information that comes in through the senses zaps through the neurons to your brain, which then interprets the information. Let's examine how information comes in through your eyes and your ears.

Light enters your eye through the **pupil**. **The iris** determines how much light gets in. The **lens**

changes its shape to focus images onto the **retina** in a process called *accommodation.* The retina has receptors called **rods** and **cones**.

- **Rods** detect black, white and gray
- **Cones** detect fine detail, and they can pick up color when there is ample light [this is why you can't see colors in the dark until your eyes adapt]

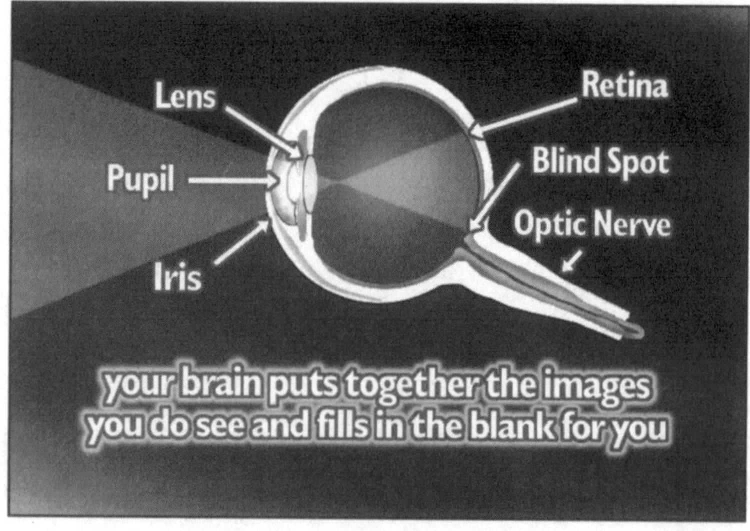

The **optic nerve** carries neural impulses from the rods and cones to the brain. Where the optic nerve leaves the eye you have a **blind spot** because there are no receptor cells there to pick up images. You don't notice the blind spot because your brain puts

together the images you do see and fills in the blanks for you. Your eye also has **feature detectors**, which are nerve cells that pick up *specific* features like movement, shape, and depth.

Now the ears:

Your **outer ear** funnels sound waves to the eardrum, which vibrates from the sound waves. The **middle ear**, which includes the *hammer*, *anvil*, and *stirrup*, amplifies and transmits the vibrations to the

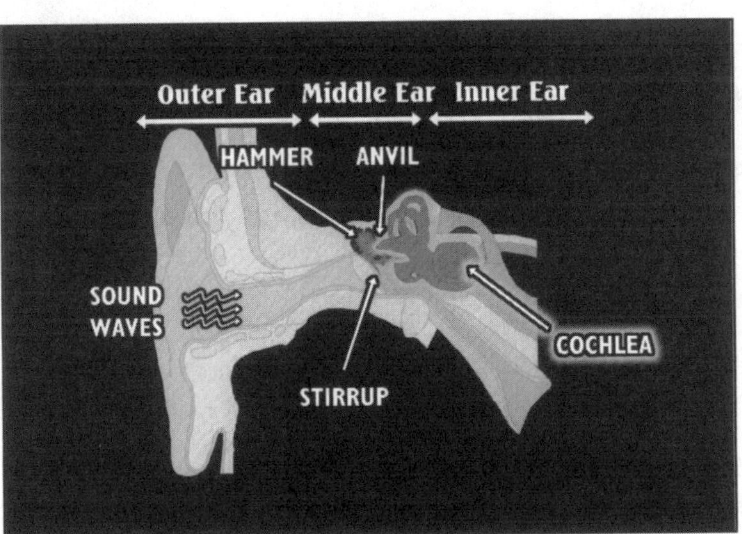

inner ear, the main part of which is called the **cochlea**.

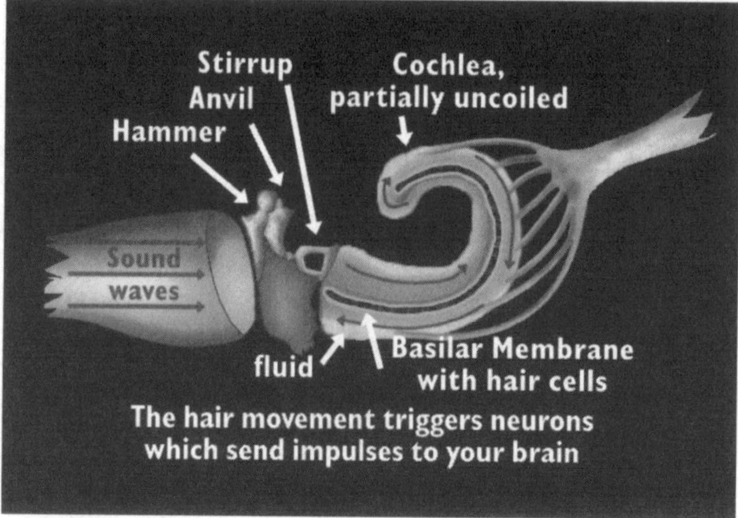

The pressure change that results from all this vibrating causes your *basilar membrane* to ripple and *hair cells* to bend. The hair movement triggers neurons which send impulses to your brain. Your brain interprets these nerve impulses and you hear.

VIDEO NOTES

Section E: Motivation

0:31:57

Motivation and emotion cause, energize and direct behavior. There are four theories which describe what motivates us:

instinct theory

drive-reduction theory

arousal theory

incentive theory

Instinct Theory:

- We're motivated by fixed behavior patterns that we don't have to learn: we eat when we're hungry, drink when we're thirsty, and go to the bathroom when we hear nature call
- Not as applicable to humans as it is to other animals, because what motivates us humans is a bit more complex than simple instincts

Drive-Reduction Theory:

- An updated version of the instinct theory that is more applicable to humans
- Discomfort associated with physiological needs,

like the need to eat, drink, and go to the bathroom, creates an aroused psychological state that drives the person to reduce the need

- Called the drive-reduction theory because it says that we are motivated by our desire to reduce the drive

Arousal Theory:

- Some behaviors come from our desire to *increase* rather than *reduce* arousal
- Humans will look for ways to increase some types of arousal, just because they like it; people will explore and learn just for the kick they get from exploring and learning
- We're driven to certain behaviors because we like them and they feel good, but they don't serve any obvious physiological need like eating and drinking
- Each individual has an optimum level of this type of stimulation that he or she enjoys

VIDEO NOTES

- If the stimulation gets to be too much, it causes tension, and the person will look for ways to reduce the stimulation and get rid of the tension

Incentive Theory:

- Takes into account the factors that lure us into an aroused state: when you smell food cooking, you may decide you want some even though you didn't feel hungry until you smelled the food

Abraham Maslow is a humanistic psychologist who developed a hierarchy of needs. **Maslow's hierarchy of needs** ranks human needs by how important they are for survival; like arousal theory and incentive theory, Maslow's hierarchy of needs tries to explain what motivates us.

According to Maslow, as you take care of the lower level needs, the higher level needs start to bug you until you satisfy them:

Study Sidekick

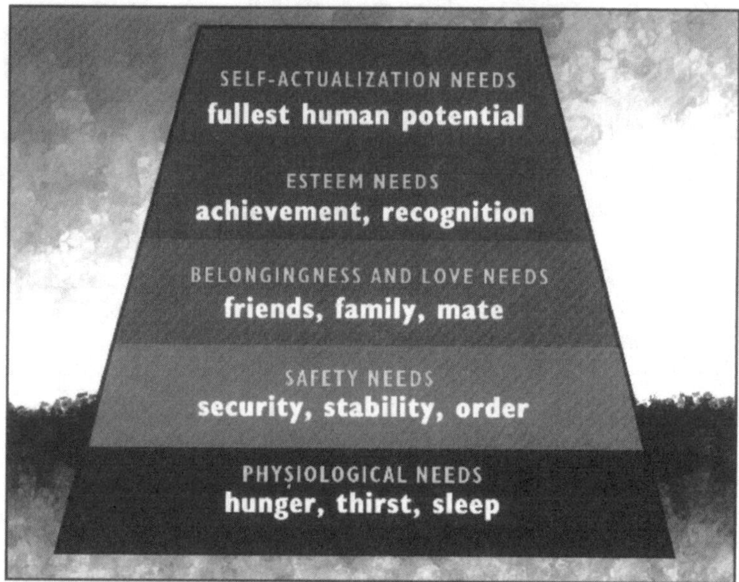

- *Physiological needs*: hunger, thirst, and sleep
- *Safety needs*: a sense of security, stability, and order
- *Belongingness and love needs*: friends, family, and a mate
- *Esteem needs*: achievement and recognition
- *Self-actualization needs*: the need to live to up to your fullest potential and really kick butt in life

VIDEO NOTES

SUMMARY

- There are lots of theories about what motivates us
- Hoss is motivated by the instinct theory; he has fixed patterns of behavior and when nature calls, he listens
- The drive-reduction theory says we eat and drink and stuff in order to reduce the discomfort caused by unsatisfied drives
- The arousal theory says we like to increase arousal if it feels good
- When you smell a chili dog and want it, that's the incentive theory talking

0:37:03

Section F: Emotion

Emotions are a combination of physiological arousal, expressive behavior, and conscious (as well as unconscious) experiences. Emotions are a combination of the stimuli you get from your senses, how you react to these stimuli, and what you think and feel at the time.

There are several theories on what actually makes a person feel emotions:

The James-Lange Theory

The Cannon-Bard Theory

Schacter's Two Factor Theory

The James-Lange theory:

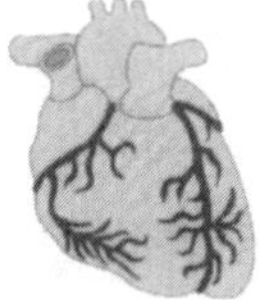

- Developed in the 1890's
- You experience emotion *after* your body responds to some stimulus
- Your body's physical response is what causes your emotion [if something happens that makes your heart pound, then you feel afraid]

Video Notes

The Cannon-Bard Theory:

- Physiological arousal, which is your body's response to a stimulus, occurs at the same time you feel emotion
- At the same time your heart starts pounding, you begin feeling scared
- The physical response does not cause the emotional feeling [it's not just the fact that your heart is pounding that causes you to feel scared]

Most modern psychologists, however, think that our memories, thoughts, and the way we interpret situations have a lot to do with how we experience emotions. So in comes:

Schacter's Two Factor Theory:

- Also known as **cognitive labeling**
- To experience emotion you have to have a physical response (one factor) and you have to be able to recognize and label that response (the other factor)

STUDY SIDEKICK

SUMMARY

- Emotions come from a combination of physiological arousal, expressive behavior, conscious, and unconscious experiences
- The James-Lange Theory: you feel emotion after your body responds to a stimulus
- The Cannon-Bard Theory: emotion occurs at the same time as the body's response to a stimulus
- Schacter's Two-Factor Theory: you have to have a physical response, and then you have to be able to recognize and label the response

?

Quiz: Part I

1) Psychology is the scientific study of __________ and __________.

2) If one attributes the development of a particular behavior to environmental conditions, rather than to heredity, one believes in the __________ approach.

3) A __________ is a testable prediction implied by a theory.

4) A test, one type of research method, needs to be both reliable, meaning that it must produce consistent and predictable results, and __________, meaning it measures what it is designed to measure.

5) What are the two settings that psychologists use to make observations? __________.

6) Which research design, or way to set up an experiment, provides the most solid conclusions when you are testing for a cause-effect relationship?

________________________________.

7) __________ are used to clearly describe the exact procedures used in an experiment.

8) Subjects become part of either an experimental group or a control group as a result of __________.

9) In a correlational study, can a researcher reliably

assert whether change in one variable caused change in the other? __________.

10) If two variables are negatively correlated, as one increases the other __________.

11) The central nervous system consists of the __________ and the __________.

12) The peripheral nervous system consists of __________ that connect the __________ to the ______________.

13) Sensory neurons carry information from __________ to the __________.

14) Motor neurons carry information from the __________ to __________.

15) __________ are the part of a neuron that receive the neural messages or impulses coming in from other neurons.

16) The __________ is a layer of fatty cells that insulates the axon. What is the axon's job? ________.

17) The space between neurons is called the __________.

18) What are two examples of neurotransmitters? _________ and __________.

19) Neurons fire according to the __________

?

QUIZ

principle.

20) The __________ of a stimulus is the smallest amount of stimulus that you can detect.

21) The __________ is the smallest difference a person can detect between two stimuli.

22) The lens of the eye focuses images onto the retina by changing its shape through a process called _________________________.

23) The point where the optic nerve leaves the eye is called the __________________.

24) __________ are nerve cells that pick up specific features like movement, shape, and depth.

25) The __________ theory suggests that the discomfort associated with physiological needs creates an aroused psychological state that drives the person to reduce the need.

26) The __________ theory asserts that some behaviors come from our desire to increase rather than decrease arousal.

27) Abraham Maslow developed a __________ which ranks human needs by how important they are for survival.

28) __________ is the need to live up to your fullest

potential.

29) The __________ theory proposes that physiological arousal occurs at the same time as the feeling of an emotion.

VIDEO NOTES

Part II: Learning and Cognition

0:39:42

Behaviorist psychologists believe that people's behavior depends on the consequences of their current and past behavior. In other words, if behavior feels good or something good happens because of it, you're probably going to do it again.

Behaviorist psychologists don't think it's important to study people's inner needs, thoughts, feelings, and motives. They go straight for the behavior, looking at how people respond to things in their environment.

People learn to associate events [when you see lightning you listen for the thunder because you know it's coming]. Associating events is called **associative learning** or **stimulus-response learning**. There are two types of associative or stimulus-response learning:

classical conditioning

operant conditioning

In classical conditioning, a stimulus from the environment triggers a response in the subject (like a rat or a human). In operant conditioning, however, the subject performs a behavior that triggers a response from the environment.

0:41:33

Section A: Classical Conditioning

The most popular example of classical conditioning is Pavlov's dog experiments. While studying how dogs digest food, Ivan Pavlov noticed that his

Hoss, the Wonder-Dog and Cerebellum mascot

dogs started drooling in *anticipation* of their food.

When the dogs saw their food bowls, heard the noises they always heard before they were fed, or even when they saw the person who usually fed them, they would salivate as if there were food right in front of them.

Video Notes

The events that normally preceded the food *elicited*, or brought out, the drooling response. This is an example of **associative learning**: the dogs associated the appearance of the dog bowls, the noises of getting the food ready, and the person who fed them with being fed.

Pavlov then conducted numerous experiments based on this observation and eventually developed a theory of associative learning. In his classic experiment, Pavlov sounded a tone just before he put meat into the dogs' mouths.

At first, the tone by itself did not get the dogs to salivate. But after a few times of pairing the tone with the meat, the dogs started to salivate when they heard the tone because they anticipated that the tone would be followed by meat. The dogs learned to associate the tone with the meat, so either the tone or the meat could make them drool. Now let's apply some terms to the experiment:

- **The Unconditioned Stimulus (UCS):** the meat that the dogs want to eat; it *naturally* elicits a response
- **The Unconditioned Response (UCR)**: the elicited response is salivation

Study Sidekick

- A **neutral stimulus** is one that, unlike the unconditioned stimulus, does *not* naturally produce a response; in Pavlov's experiments, the **neutral stimulus** is the tone
- Once the dogs paired the sound of the tone with the meat and started to salivate just at the sound of the tone, the tone is no longer a neutral stimulus
- The dogs were taught, or *conditioned*, to salivate at the sound of the tone, so the tone becomes the **conditioned stimulus (CS)**
- The dogs' salivating in response to the tone is the **conditioned response (CR)**

The other famous case of classical conditioning is the story of Little Albert and the experimenter (tormentor) John Watson. Little Albert, like a lot of young kids, was naturally afraid of loud noises, but not white rats.

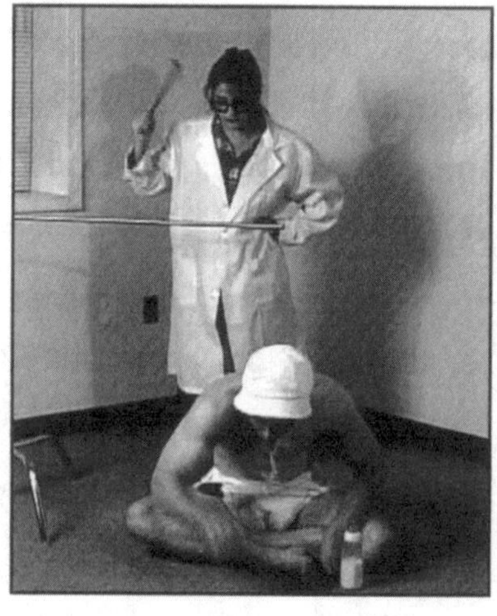

Video Notes

Watson put Little Albert into a room with a white rat and just as Little Albert was reaching out to touch it, Watson smashed a hammer against a steel bar right behind his head. After only a few pairings of the sound and the rat, Little Albert burst into tears upon seeing the rat. A few days later, poor Little Albert burst into tears any time he spotted a white dog, a white rabbit, or a white fur coat.

Let's break it down for you:

- **Unconditioned stimulus (UCS):** the loud noise; it naturally elicits a response
- **Unconditioned response (UCR):** Little Albert's fear of the loud noise (because he is naturally afraid of it)
- **Conditioned stimulus (CS):** the rat; Little Albert was not naturally afraid of rats--he was conditioned to be afraid of rats
- **Conditioned response (CR):** Little Albert's conditioned fear of the rat

(By the way, today, such an experiment is considered highly unethical and would never be conducted. Put your hammers and iron bars away, you weirdos.)

Study Sidekick

Here are some more things you should know about classical conditioning:

The first phase of classical conditioning learning is called **acquisition**. **Acquisition** is the time period in which the unconditioned stimulus becomes associated with the conditioned stimulus.

- The acquisition period for Little Albert is the time it took him to associate the loud noise (UCS) with white rats (CS)

Once the response is conditioned, **generalization** may occur. **Generalization** is the tendency for things similar to the conditioned stimulus to cause a response that's similar to the conditioned response.

- When Little Albert freaked out at the sight of a white fur coat, he was generalizing his conditioned fear of white rats to white fur coats

Discrimination is the ability to tell the difference between similar stimuli.

- If Watson had someone wearing a fur coat come and play with Little Albert, and if Watson didn't whack the steel bar while Little Albert played, the poor little boy would have

Video Notes

eventually learned to discriminate between the white rat and other white furry objects

Extinction is the process of getting rid of a conditioned response.

- You can make a conditioned response go away if you present the conditioned stimulus (a rat) a whole bunch of times without following it with the unconditioned stimulus (a loud, scary noise)
- The term extinction is a little bit misleading because the association of the unconditioned stimulus (the loud noise) with the conditioned stimulus (the rat) does not become *extinct,* it becomes *suppressed*--it doesn't really go away completely

Little Albert may all of a sudden start freaking out again at the sight of a rat even though the rat hasn't been associated with the noise for quite awhile. This is called **spontaneous recovery**. This whole experiment is totally demented.

SUMMARY

- The unconditioned stimulus naturally and automatically elicits a response
- An unconditioned response is a response that a subject gives naturally, without having to learn anything
- A neutral stimulus doesn't naturally produce any response at all
- Once a neutral stimulus is associated with an unconditioned stimulus and starts to produce a response, it becomes a conditioned stimulus; the subject has been conditioned to respond to it
- A conditioned response is a response that has been learned, like the dogs learning to salivate at the sound of a tone; it's not something they would do naturally

Section B: Operant Conditioning

0:52:50

Operant conditioning teaches subjects to associate behaviors with their *consequences*. The subject acts first, and then the environment responds with consequences to that action. Remember, this is different from classical conditioning, in which a stimulus from the environment triggers a response in the subject.

According to the principles of operant conditioning, behaviors are more likely to be repeated if they are followed by a reward, or something that would provide an incentive to do it again. Conversely, behaviors are less likely to be repeated if they are followed by punishment.

The principles of acquisition, extinction, spontaneous recovery, generalization, and discrimination all apply to operant conditioning as well as to classical conditioning.

Operant conditioning is practically synonymous with the work of B.F. Skinner, who expanded **Thorndike's law of effect**, which says that rewarded behavior is likely to recur.

Skinner designed the **Skinner box**--a chamber containing a bar that an animal can press to obtain a

food pellet and a device to record the animal's rate of bar pressing.

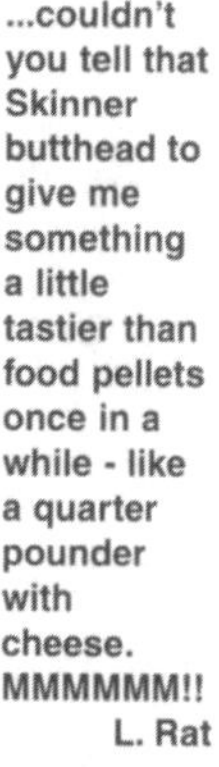
...couldn't you tell that Skinner butthead to give me something a little tastier than food pellets once in a while - like a quarter pounder with cheese. MMMMMM!!
L. Rat

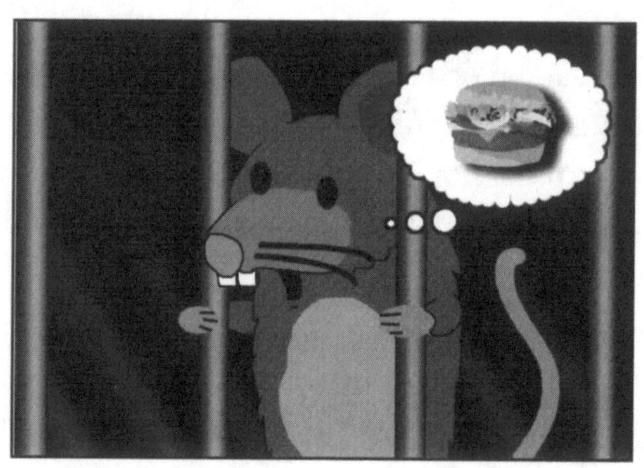

Skinner used his box to experiment with animals like rats and pigeons. He was trying to see if he could teach them to do weird behaviors in order to get a reward (food). The animal would typically have to press a bar (which is a weird behavior for a rat or a bird) in order to get a food pellet.

To get animals to perform like he wanted them to, like getting the rats to press the bar in the Skinner box, Skinner used **shaping**, which is the process of rewarding behaviors that come close to the behavior he was looking for.

Behaviors that come close to and lead up to the

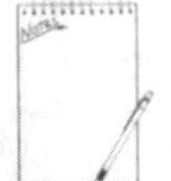

desired behavior are called **successive approximations**.

For example, if you want to shape bar-pressing behavior in rats, you start by rewarding a natural behavior. When the rat goes near the bar, you give it a food pellet. Once the rat has learned that going near the bar results in a reward, then you only reward it when it touches the bar, and so on and so on until the desired behavior is learned.

to hell with it...let's play poker!!!
L. Rat

Rewards in operant conditioning are specifically called **reinforcers**. However, not all reinforcers are like rewards. **Primary reinforcers** are rewards--they're naturally satisfying, like food. **Secondary reinforcers**, on the other hand, are not naturally sat-

isfying; subjects have to *learn* that secondary reinforcers are worth repeating a behavior for.

For example, an animal can learn that a light signals food (the primary reinforcer) and consequently the light (the secondary reinforcer) becomes reinforcing. People use things like money, grades, and praise as secondary reinforcers.

All the reinforcement we've talked about so far is called **positive reinforcement**. Positive reinforcement *gives* the subject something to make it more likely that a behavior will be repeated.

There is also **negative reinforcement**, which is not what we typically think of as a reward, but it does make the subject want to repeat the behavior. Negative reinforcement "reinforces" behavior by *taking away* something unpleasant or aversive. A rat in a Skinner box may learn that pressing the bar stops the electrical current that's going through the floor of the box. This is negative reinforcement because the bar-pressing behavior is reinforced when the pain of the electrical current stops.

Negative reinforcement is often confused with punishment, but it's really not at all like punishment.

Video Notes

In the case of reinforcement, don't think of the terms negative as bad and positive as good. Remember that positive reinforcement means giving something good to increase the likelihood of a behavior, and negative reinforcement means taking away something that's bad to increase the likelihood of a behavior. Both positive and negative reinforcement increase the likelihood of a behavior occurring.

Punishment is something that *discourages* the subject from repeating a behavior.

Punishment, however, is an unpleasant event that decreases the likelihood that a behavior will occur. Overall, punishment is not very effective. Punished behavior becomes suppressed but not forgotten.

For example, if a kid gets spanked for picking his nose, he may just make sure he doesn't do it again around his parents. Instead he may do it in a safe atmosphere, where no authority figures can catch him. Also, punishment often backfires and winds up increasing unwanted responses, like fear and aggression. Most importantly, punishment doesn't encourage desired behaviors.

SUMMARY

- There are two types of associative or stimulus-response learning: classical conditioning and operant conditioning
- Classical conditioning: the environment provides a stimulus, and the subject responds; Pavlov's dogs heard the tone first, then they started to salivate
- Operant conditioning: the subject acts first, then the environment responds; if the subject likes the response, it will probably repeat the behavior
  - In the case of Skinner's rats, the rat presses the bar first, then it gets a food pellet
  - Since the rat likes the food pellet, it will press the bar again

VIDEO NOTES

Section C: Social Learning

1:00:14

People can learn by making associations, but they can also learn through **observation:** watching and imitating the behavior of others. You don't have to personally experience something to learn about it. The process of learning through observation is called **modeling**.

Albert Bandura studied how children learn to model behavior. Bandura's classic study involved having children sit in a room and play. At the same time, an adult kicked and hit an inflated Bobo doll while screaming, "Knock him down! Sock it to him!"

Next, the children were deliberately frustrated by not being allowed to play with their favorite toys. After the children became good and mad, they were sent to another room with a few toys and a Bobo doll.

These children (as compared to children not exposed to the adult's behavior) kicked, hit, and screamed at the Bobo doll in the same way that the adult did.

Besides contributing to learning theory, Bandura's study also helps us understand the behavior of children that come from abusive families. These chil-

dren are often violent and end up abusing themselves and/or others because they learned the behavior by watching their parents.

Section D: Memory and Forgetting

1:01:34

Information processing begins with **encoding**: getting information into your brain from your sensory receptors. The next step is **storing**--retaining the information in your brain. The final step is **retrieving**, which involves getting information back out of your brain.

Encoding can occur through **automatic processing** or **effortful processing**:

- **Automatic processing**: pretty effortless; when you read a word, you already know what it means
- **Effortful processing**: encoding that requires concentration and conscious thought (like when you agonize over your calculus homework)

There are two ways you encode information:

- One way is through **rehearsal**, just repeating the information. One way is through **rehearsal**, just repeating the information.
- We also encode information by visualizing it or making a mental picture of it; visualizing

information is called **imagery**

Once you encode the information you have to organize it to make it easier for your memory to hang on to. You can organize encoded information through **chunking**: organizing info into familiar, manageable units.

- Phone numbers are organized into chunks so you can remember them better. Although technically the string of numbers in the chunked phone number is no different than the continuous string, the one that is broken up and made familiar is easier to remember. For example, it's much easier to remember **1-800-VCR-REVU** than **18008277388.**
- Forming **hierarchies** is a higher level of chunking that's a lot like developing outlines. When you develop a hierarchy, you organize information into main categories that are further organized into subcategories.

Sensory memory is the first place information goes as it comes in through the senses. Next, the information is briefly stored in the **short-term memory** until it is either forgotten or sent to the **long term memory**, which is a limitless and relatively perma-

nent storehouse of information.

Short term memory (STM) can only store seven chunks of information (plus or minus two) and then it fills up. That's why random phone numbers are easy to remember for a little while.

Unless the information is worked in some way (encoded) and consequently transferred to the **long term memory**, it will **decay** (be forgotten). The long-term memory has an unlimited capacity for retention; however, access to everything "remembered" is not always available.

Forgetting, or **retrieval failure**, occurs through **interference**, which is when learning one set of material interferes with remembering another. There are two types of interference:

Proactive interference

Retroactive interference

- **Proactive interference:** prior learning interferes with learning new information, like when the French you learned in high school gets in the way of the Spanish you're trying to learn in college

- **Retroactive interference:** newly learned information interferes with previously learned information, like when reading chapter nine makes you forget what you learned in chapter eight

Section E: Cognitive Development and Jean Piaget

Cognitive development is the development of all mental activities that have to do with thinking, knowing, and remembering. ***Jean Piaget*** studied human cognitive development and created a theory based on his belief that intellectual development occurs as humans struggle to make sense of the world. According to Piaget, in order to make sense of the world, humans form concepts called **schemas**.

Schemas are organized sets of thoughts or actions, like the set of actions you follow to make your bed or tie your shoe. If you learn a new way to make your bed or tie your shoe, you have to change your existing schema. This happens in two ways:

assimilation

accommodation

Assimilation:

- Fitting new information into the framework of what you already know
- It's like taking in new experiences and making sense of them based on old experiences; Little

Susie might know a cow is a big, hairy, four-legged animal, so to Little Susie that means all big, hairy, four-legged animals are cows

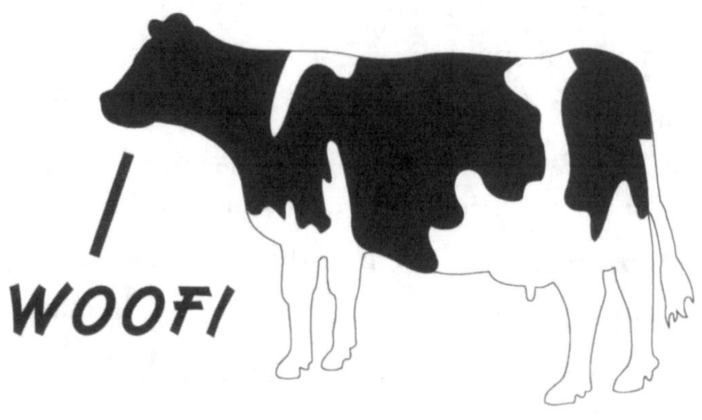

Accommodation:

- Sometimes you can't make sense of a new experience based on what you already know. Sometimes you have to *change* your existing schema to fit new information or experiences. This process is called **accommodation.**
- When Little Susie figures out that a horse is a horse, of course, and not a cow, she has changed her existing framework of understanding to **accommodate** the fact that not all big, hairy, four-legged creatures are cows.

VIDEO NOTES

Piaget outlined four stages of cognitive development:

sensorimotor stage

preoperational stage

concrete operational stage

formal operational stage

The Sensorimotor Stage:

- From birth to 2 years
- Children understand the world primarily through their senses and by physically dealing with things
- Kids develop **object permanence**: the awareness that objects exist even when they can't see them [Once this happens, peek-a-boo isn't nearly as exciting because the kid knows that even though you're hiding behind the pillow, you're really still there.]
- **Stranger anxiety** develops: kids start to detect a difference between loved ones and strangers, and they freak out when a stranger tries to hold them or do something with them (wreaking havoc for baby-sitters everywhere)

The Preoperational Stage:

- From the ages of two and six
- Kids in this stage understand a little bit more about the world than what's in front of them at the moment
- They develop language abilities: if you say the word "ball" to a preoperational child, she will be able to picture a ball in her mind, even though there isn't a ball in front of her
- Kids in the preoperational stage don't understand the concept of *conservation*: the principle that properties such as mass, volume, and numbers remain the same despite changes in their form
- Preoperational children are **egocentric**: unable to perceive things from another person's point of view

The Concrete Operational Stage:

- From seven to eleven years
- Children become able to think logically in situations that are not abstract
- They understand the concept of conservation and they are able to do mathematical operations

Video Notes

- A concrete operational kid can figure out that two one-inch pieces of cake don't add up to more cake than one two-inch piece
- If you throw in an abstract concept, however, things go bad for the concrete operational kid. If you ask a kid, "how much freedom is too much?" the kid will likely be confused and just think you're weird.

The Formal Operational Stage:

- Begins around age 12 and continues into adulthood
- In this stage, you can do abstract reasoning, figure out the consequences of actions and events and think about moral issues

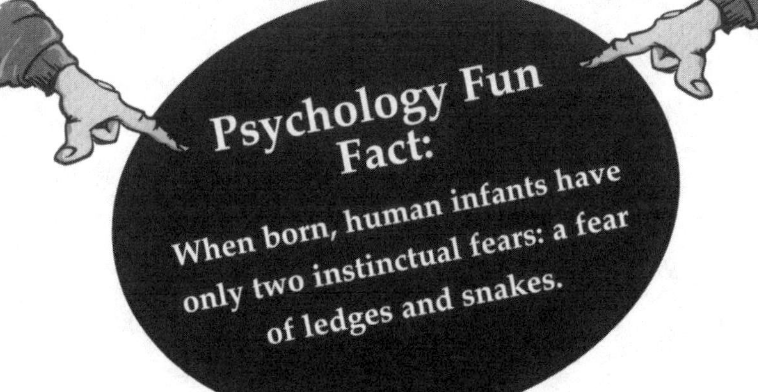

SUMMARY

- According to Jean Piaget, humans make sense of the world by forming organized sets of actions he called schemas
- When we learn new things, we have to adjust our existing schemas
- We do this through assimilation, which is fitting new information into our existing schema, and accommodation, which is changing our schema to fit the new information
- Piaget outlined four stages of cognitive development:
    - The sensorimotor stage: children understand the world primarily through their senses
    - The preoperational stage: children develop language and object permanence
    - The concrete operational stage: kids learn to think logically, do math, and they grasp the concept of conservation
    - The formal operational stage: children can do abstract reasoning, figure out consequences, and think about moral issues

?

QUIZ: Part II

1) Expecting to hear thunder after seeing lightning is an example of __________ learning.

2) In Pavlov's classic study, the meat was the unconditioned stimulus. Before Pavlov paired the tone and the meat together, the tone was the __________. After the tone became associated with the meat, the tone was the __________.

3) The time period in which the UCS becomes associated with the CS is called __________.

4) __________ is the tendency for things similar to the CS to cause a response that's similar to the CR.

5) The term extinction, which is the process of getting rid of a conditioned response, is actually a bit misleading because the CR does not become extinct, it becomes __________.

6) In operant conditioning, __________ is the rewarding of successive approximations, that is, the rewarding of behaviors that come close to the behavior that the researcher is trying to condition.

7) __________ reinforcement is reinforcement that gives the subject something to make it more likely that a behavior will be repeated.

8) __________ reinforcement is reinforcement that takes away something unpleasant or aversive to make it more likely that a behavior will be repeated.

9) __________ is an unpleasant event that discourages the subject from repeating a behavior.

10) Learning through observation, that is, watching and imitating the behavior of others is called __________.

11) One way of encoding information, getting information into your brain, is through __________, organizing information into familiar, manageable units.

12) __________ memory can only store 7 plus or minus 2 chunks of information and then it __________.

13) __________ occurs when newly learned information interferes with previously learned information.

14) __________ is the development of all mental activities that have to do with thinking, knowing, and remembering.

15) __________ is fitting new information into the framework of what you already know.

16) A child who primarily tries to understand the

?

Quiz

world through his/her senses is in the __________ stage. During this stage, children develop __________ which is the awareness that objects exist even though they can't see them. During this stage, children also develop __________, which occurs as children become able to detect a difference between loved ones and strangers.

17) Children who do not understand the concept of conservation are in the __________ stage. Children in this stage are also __________, unable to perceive things from another person's point of view.

18) A child in the __________ stage can reason abstractly, figure out the consequences of actions, and even think about moral issues.

1:16:04

Part III: Social and Personality Development

1:16:08

Section A: Social Development

Social development occurs in relation to our attachments to other people. We learn to function socially (as a part of a group) so we'll be accepted and allowed to hang out with other people.

Attachment is a survival impulse. If we can create emotional ties with other people, those people will help us meet our needs, and we will have a better chance of surviving.

Harry Harlow's famous study of monkeys shows the need for attachment. Harlow raised baby monkeys, giving them each two artificial mothers.

Video Notes

One artificial mom was shaped like a monkey but was made of wire. This “mother” had a bottle sticking out of it, so it provided food to the baby monkeys. The other “mother” was also made of wire and shaped like a monkey, but it was covered with soft terry cloth. This fake monkey mom didn’t provide food or anything, but the baby monkeys overwhelmingly preferred it anyway. They cuddled with it, clung to it when they were frightened, and always returned to it after they’d been out exploring.

The babies only went to the uncovered wire mom when they were hungry. After they ate, it was right to back to the terry cloth mom for comfort.

STUDY SIDEKICK

Attachment seems to be related to reassuring, pleasant, tactile stimuli.

We can apply this study to people. Starting when we're babies, we need to develop a sense of **basic trust**--a sense that the world is a safe place and that there will be others around us who care about us, about how we feel, and whether or not we're happy and doing well.

If we don't start feeling this sense of basic trust when we're babies, it's hard to develop social skills, self-esteem, hope, and faith when we're older.

VIDEO NOTES

Section B: The Social Theory

1:18:12

People are always trying to understand and explain everyone else's behavior. We try to associate their actions with something that we think may cause them to act that way. Psychologists call our tendency to figure each other out the **attribution theory.** We might attribute, or associate, people's behaviors with their internal characteristics, like their kindness, impatience, cruelty, or whatever. This is called **dispositional attribution**. Think dispositional: we blame it on their disposition.

Or we might associate their behavior with external characteristics (what's going on in the environment around them) like their living conditions (such as a wealthy or abusive family). This is called **situational attribution**. Think situational: we blame it on the situation.

When we try to figure out why a person does what he does, it's easy to make a **fundamental attribution error**, which is the tendency to underestimate the impact of a person's situation and overestimate the impact of that person's disposition.

When we're explaining our own behavior, we often have a **self-serving bias**; we explain our own

good behaviors in terms of our own good internal attributes, and we blame our bad behaviors on the environment and other external things.

When other people have problems or get in trouble, however, we tend to blame their *internal* characteristics. In other words, we assume they did something to cause their own misfortune. This tendency is called the **just world hypothesis**--the tendency of people to believe the world is just. (People therefore get what they deserve and deserve what they get.)

There are some flaws in this logic, of course, since people who do well are not necessarily the most deserving, and people who don't do well aren't necessarily evil. It's kind of like saying that people who are abused deserve the abuse, and people who get athlete's foot deserve the affliction.

If you believe that people deserve what they get, it's easy to develop stereotypes and prejudices against the less wealthy and successful groups in society. It's important to think about how you explain your own and other people's actions, because the *attitudes* you develop about yourself and others influence the actions you take.

Our attitudes, beliefs, decisions, and actions are,

to a large extent, based on the influence of others. This happens because of the human tendency towards **conformity**, which is adjusting your behavior or thinking to coincide with a group standard.

Social psychologists think that prejudices develop from the tendency to favor your own group over others, a tendency they call **in-group bias. In-group bias** can lead to **scapegoating**, which is when you or your group blame some injustice on another group, just because it's convenient to blame the other group. People outside your own group are an easy outlet for anger. Just being in a crowd can make you act differently than you would if you were by yourself. A well-trained athlete will likely perform even better in front of an audience than she would training by herself. This is called **social facilitation**. The idea is that the social situation facilitates the behavior.

But social facilitation only works with behaviors you're already familiar with. If you try something that you've never done before in front of a crowd, you're liable to look like a big fool. **Social loafing** is the tendency for an individual in a group to exert less effort in group activities when the group will be held accountable for whatever happens but the individual doesn't have to bear responsibility himself.

SUMMARY

- When we associate people's behavior with their internal attributes, it's called dispositional attribution
- When we associate behaviors with external forces, it's called situational attribution
- The tendency to overestimate the impact of a person's disposition and underestimate the impact of external forces is called a fundamental attribution error
- When we blame the environment for the things we do wrong rather than taking responsibility for our own actions, that's called self-serving bias
- The just world hypothesis is the belief that the world is fair, and people get exactly what they deserve
- In-group bias is the tendency to favor your own group over others
- Scapegoating is blaming other groups for injustices, not because it is necessarily their fault, but because it is easy and convenient to

VIDEO NOTES

blame them

- Social facilitation helps us perform familiar behaviors better in front of a crowd than we would in private
- Social loafing allows us to exert less effort personally when we know that the entire group we're in will be held responsible for whatever actions are taken

Art Plinko of Psycho Jackpot

1:25:10

Section C: Personality Development

Distinctive patterns of thinking, feeling, and behaving form personality. We'll look at three theories of personality:

psychoanalytic

humanistic

social-cognitive

Be aware that there are other theories of personality besides the ones we will go over. You already learned about one when we talked about Skinner. Behaviorism definitely applies to personality, since our personalities reflect which of our behaviors get reinforced. But since you already have a good idea of what learning theories and behaviorism are all about, we won't go over them again.

The Psychoanalytic Theory:

- Developed by ***Sigmund Freud***
- Unconscious motivations influence personality development

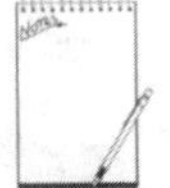

Video Notes

- The stuff that's going on in your head that you're not aware of has a lot to do with how you think and act
- The **unconscious** controls most of our behaviors and is comprised of thoughts, wishes, feelings, and memories that have been repressed from consciousness because they are anxiety-arousing
- Even though we are not aware of what our unconscious thoughts are, however, they have a powerful influence on the everyday decisions we make, like decisions we make about our professions, mates, and habits
- Unconscious thoughts also have an influence on symptoms we develop when we're psychologically distressed

"The 'feel good' movie of the year!"
-Sigmund Freud commenting on *The Stimulating World of Psychology*

Personality develops as a result of conflict between people's pleasure-seeking and aggressive impulses as well as the way their desires for pleasure and aggression fit into society's rules.

The conflict that develops between our innate desires and the rules of society are represented as three structures of the mind:

the id

the ego

the superego

According to the **pleasure principle**, the **id** is wholly unconscious and seeks immediate gratification of sexual and aggressive needs. The **ego** tries to meet the needs of the id the best it can without letting the id run wild and wreak havoc. The ego

operates under the **reality principle**, keeping desires realistic and under control so they bring long-term pleasure instead of pain and chaos. The ego medi-

Video Notes

ates between the wild desires of the id and the restraints imposed by the **superego**:

- A conscience that represents society's norms and values
- The superego goes one step beyond the ego by considering not only the real, but also the ideal
- The superego thinks about how we *ought* to behave according to our society
- It uses ideas about morality that come from our parents and our environment and gives us a strong sense of right and wrong
- Can make us feel very proud or very guilty
- Often opposes the id

The **ego** works really hard to reconcile the id and the superego.

According to Freud, a person's personality forms during the early childhood years. Freud outlined a series of **psychosexual stages** that children pass through as the pleasure-seeking energies of the id are transferred to **erogenous zones**, pleasure-sensitive areas of the body. The psychosexual stages are:

the oral stage

the anal stage

the phallic stage

the latency stage

the genital stage

<u>The Oral Stage:</u>

- A child is in the **oral stage** from birth to approximately 18 months
- She gets most of her pleasure from sucking, biting and chewing
- During this stage she is still completely dependent on her mother

<u>The Anal Stage:</u>

- A child is in the **anal stage** from about 18 months to three years
- During this stage, a child gains a sense of control over the environment as his mother toilet trains him
- Called the anal stage because pleasure comes from the use of his bladder and sphincter muscles

- He knows that when he uses these muscles he can control part of his environment and is no longer totally dependent on his mother

The Phallic Stage:

- A child is in the phallic stage from about three to six years
- Pleasurable feelings are mostly associated with the genitals
- At this age a child feels sexually attracted to his opposite sex parent and

feels jealous of his same sex parent

- This complex state of affairs is known as the **Oedipus complex** for boys and the **Electra complex** for girls

The Oedipus Complex:

◆ During the phallic stage, boys develop sexual desires for Mom and murderous feelings for poor Dad

◆ Boys feel guilty for wanting to off Dad, and they're afraid he might want to retaliate

◆ Boys develop castration anxiety

The Electra Complex:

◆ During the phallic stage, girls develop penis envy, feeling that the penis is the superior sex organ

◆ Because of this penis envy, girls develop a desire for Dad and want to get Mom out of the picture

Luckily, humans get a break from these problems

between the ages of six and puberty, during the **latency stage**.

The Latency Stage:

- From about six years to puberty (11 or 12)
- A child's sexual desires become dormant
- Id energies focus on developing same-sex peer relationships and pursuing academic endeavors

The Genital Stage:

- From puberty to adulthood
- Involves relating to others in a sexually mature way
- There is strong sexual attraction to others
- Pleasure is mostly associated with the genitals

At any point during development, the child may become **fixated** on pleasures associated with a particular stage. Fixation occurs as a result of either getting too much or too little pleasure during that stage. Someone fixated on the oral stage might become a chain smoker. Someone fixated on the anal stage

might become really messy and disorganized, a condition known as being anal expulsive. A person may become anal retentive, which is characterized by being uptight and controlling.

As a result of living in a civilized world, our instinctual urges (id impulses) cannot always be fully satisfied. When the ego's control over id impulses becomes threatened, we feel anxious and protect ourselves through the use of **defense mechanisms:**

repression

regression

reaction formation

projection

rationalization

displacement

sublimation

Since all **defense mechanisms** reduce or redirect anxiety by distorting or denying reality, all defenses are a form of **denial**, which is the unconscious refusal to accept reality.

Video Notes

Repression: involves banishing anxiety-arousing thoughts, feelings, and memories from consciousness, like the guy who had to repress any memories of his fish after it died

Regression: retreating to an earlier stage of development, like the boy who picks up thumb-sucking again on the first day of college

Reaction formation: the switching of unacceptable impulses into their opposites; for example, fervent activists might be fighting against their own strong impulses that they want to deny

Projection: people disguise their own threatening impulses by pinning them on other people; if you really can't stand someone, but you don't want to admit it, you may claim that that person hates you

Rationalization: you justify your actions and cover up the real, unconscious reasons for doing them; for example, an alcoholic who claims he's drinking just to be sociable is rationalizing

Displacement: you take your anger (or some other unacceptable feeling or impulse) and divert it from its source to something or someone else; for example, a man who is angry at his boss may come home and kick his dog

Sublimation: re-channeling unacceptable impulses into socially acceptable stuff like art

VIDEO NOTES

SUMMARY

- The psychoanalytic theory proposes that unconscious motivations influence personality development
- The mind has three components: the id, the ego and the superego
- Five stages of development that we go through as we grow up:
  - The oral stage, when pleasure comes from sucking and biting
  - The anal stage, when pleasure comes from using the bladder and sphincter muscles
  - The phallic stage, when pleasure comes from self stimulation of the genitals
  - The latency stage, when sexual feelings recede a bit and we develop an identification with our same sex parent
  - The genital stage, when pleasure comes from the genitals and mature sexual relationships
- If we get too much or too little pleasure in any

of these stages, we can become fixated on that stage and focus too much on the pleasures associated with that stage

- When our drives and desires get out of control, we may use one or more defense mechanisms, which are all a form of denial, to protect ourselves

Velma:
"Now we'll find out who the ego really is....(tearing off the rubber mask)... Mr. Jenkins!"

Shaggy:
"Zoinks! Mr. Jenkins! You're my id?!"

Mr. Jenkins:
"Ah, and I woulda pulled it off, too, if it weren't for my meddling superego and that pesky dog!"

VIDEO NOTES

Section D: The Humanistic and Social-Cognitive Theories

The Humanistic Theory:

Abraham Maslow and ***Carl Rogers*** each developed his own theory of personality that focuses on human potential.

In **Maslow's humanistic theory of personality,** self-actualization is the ultimate psychological need. **Self-actualization** arises after basic physical and psychological needs are met and self-esteem is achieved. The drive for self-actualization is the motivation to fulfill your potential--to become everything you can and want to be.

According to **Roger's humanistic theory of personality**, self-actualization will occur all by itself unless somehow circumstances or the environment get in the way. In order for self-actualization tendencies to be realized, people must fulfill certain requirements. They must be:

- *Genuine*, completely open with their feelings
- *Accepting*, showing an **unconditional positive regard** by embracing others regardless of their failures
- *Empathic*, non-judgmental in their disclosure of feelings

1:38:18

Social Cognitive Theory:

The social cognitive theory is somewhat comparable to Skinner and the behaviorists. This theory emphasizes the importance of a person's environment. Psychologists that adhere to this theory believe that people learn patterns of behavior through conditioning and modeling.

But social cognitive theorists take all this one step further. They focus on how people *think* and how their interpretations of what's going on around them

affect their responses, a view called **reciprocal determinism. Reciprocal determinism** deals with the way personality interacts with the environment. Social-cognitive psychologists believe that your sense of **personal control**, having control over your environment rather than feeling helpless, is an important determinant of personality.

Some people have an **external locus of control:** a belief that forces outside their personal control, like luck or the will of others, determine their fates. Some people have an **internal locus of control:** the belief that they control their own fates.

There are gender differences associated with locus of control: men tend to blame external factors for failure and internal factors for success, whereas women tend to blame internal factors for failure and external factors for success.

SUMMARY

- Humanists believe that humans are basically good, and we all have a natural drive for self-actualization, to become everything we can and want to be
- To reach self-actualization, you have to be genuine, empathic, and have unconditional positive regard for others
- Social-cognitive theorists focus on reciprocal determinism, or the way personality interacts with the environment
- They believe that a sense of personal control is an important factor in personality
- People who feel that forces outside their personal control determine their fates have an external locus of control
- People who believe they control their own fates have an internal locus of control

Section E: Abnormal Psychology

1:40:46

A **psychological disorder** is a condition in which a person exhibits behavior that is judged to be atypical, disturbing, unjustifiable, and maladaptive. There are several different psychological disorders, which we touch on below.

Somatoform disorders: psychological disorders that physically affect the body

Conversion disorder:

- A type of somatoform disorder
- A person has real physical symptoms, but there's no apparent physical reason for the problem
- Example: a soldier who, although his wounds are cured, can't move his legs and can't go back into battle

Dissociative disorders: conscious awareness becomes dissociated (separated) from previous memories, thoughts, and feelings. In other words, you lose your past.

Amnesia:

Study Sidekick

- A dissociative disorder
- Patients lose either all of their memories or they lose the parts of their memories that are associated with a situation that made them anxious and upset, like a horrible accident

Fugue states:

- Amnesia accompanied by a flight from home and identity
- Patients lose their memories, leave their homes and the lives they've known, and take off for somewhere else

Multiple personality disorder:

- Patient exhibits two or more separate personalities and alternates back and forth between personalities
- One personality may or may not be aware of the existence of the other personalities
- Condition usually results from a childhood trauma, such as sexual abuse
- Multiple personality disorder is very rare

[Since the release of "The Stimulating World of Psychology," the name for Multiple Personality

Disorder has been changed to Dissociative Identity Disorder. This change occurred with the introduction of the Diagnostic and Statistical Manual of Mental Disorders-IV.]

Anxiety Disorder: patient has a persistent, distressing anxiety

Generalized anxiety disorder:

- Sufferers are continually tense, apprehensive, and in a state of autonomic nervous system arousal--they often have a racing heart, sweaty palms, stomach butterflies, and a hard time sleeping
- Patients usually don't know what they are so anxious about and so don't know what to do to relieve the situation

FEAR

Phobic disorder: a persistent, irrational fear of a specific object or situation

Obsessive-compulsive disorder patients usually exhibit two symptoms, **obsessions** and **compulsions**:

Obsessions:

- Unwanted, unreasonable, repetitive thoughts which the patient absolutely cannot get out of her head
- Patient often becomes obsessed with the thought that she will act in an inappropriate manner, that she will swear in public or make obscene gestures

Compulsions:

- Acts that a patient performs over and over, such as washing ones hands or checking to make sure that a door is locked over and over

Obsessive-compulsive people may be obsessed with cleanliness or the possibility of something tragic happening. They may be compelled to wash their hands 100 times a day or repeat rituals like walking in and out of a doorway, checking to see if locks are locked, and ovens are off.

Mood disorders: characterized by emotional extremes

Major depressive disorder:

- May experience two or more weeks of

depressed moods, feelings of worthlessness, and diminished interest in most activities

- Depression can come from anger or guilt that the depressed person turns in on himself, or it may come from losing an object or a loved one
- Depressed feelings may also come from *learned helplessness*--the feeling that you can't do anything to alleviate the pain or make your life better
- Depressed people tend to explain bad events in terms that are stable ("it's going to last forever")
- They describe bad events as *global* ("it's going to affect everything I do") and *internal* ("it's all my fault")

Bipolar disorder:

- Patient alternates between the hopelessness and stagnation of depression (see definition above) and the overexcited state of *mania,* which is characterized by euphoria, hyperactivity, and a grandiose sense of optimism
- Involves a chemical imbalance in the brain

- People with the disorder may have a genetic predisposition for it

Personality disorders: impair social functioning

Several types of personality disorders:

paranoid

narcissistic

antisocial

- A **paranoid** person is excessively suspicious and guarded, unable to trust others, and tends to be hostile

- A **narcissistic** person has an exaggerated sense of privilege and grandiosity and expects to be catered to and admired by all
- An **antisocial** person doesn't seem to have a conscience and feels no remorse for hurting others, even loved ones

Schizophrenia:

- A severe disorder characterized by a "split" from reality
- Suffer from:

VIDEO NOTES

- *Delusions:* disorganized and confused thinking
- *Hallucinations:* disturbed visions and perceptions
- Inappropriate emotions and behaviors
- A withdrawal from the world

• Drugs that block dopamine receptors have been successful in decreasing schizophrenic symptoms

QUIZ: Part III

1) Harry Harlow's study of baby monkeys' reactions to two artificial monkey mothers made out of wire: one with a bottle sticking out of it, and one wrapped in a soft terry cloth, was an attempt to show that __________ is a basic human need.

2) A sense that the world is a safe place and that there will be people around us who care about us is called a sense of __________.

3) The attribution of people's behaviors to internal characteristics is called __________ attribution.

4) The __________ is the tendency to underestimate the impact of the situation and overestimate the impact of a person's disposition.

5) The __________ is when we explain our own good behaviors in terms of our own good internal attributes, and we blame our bad behaviors on the environment.

"So I'm sitting in a bar with Charlie Manson and he says, 'Hey, is it hot in here or am I just *^%$&# crazy?'"
-C. Paucek

6) When other people have problems or get in trouble, we tend to blame their internal characteristics, in other words, we assume they did something to cause their own misfortune. This is called the __________.

7) __________ is the blaming of some injustice on

?

Quiz

another group.

8) __________ is the tendency for people in a group to exert less effort when the "group" will be held accountable for whatever happens.

9) __________ theory proposes that unconscious motivations influence personality development.

10) The __________ is wholly unconscious and seeks immediate gratification of sexual and aggressive needs according to the __________.

11) The __________ tries to meet the needs of the id the best it can without letting it run wild and wreak havoc according to the __________.

12) The __________ is like a conscience that represents society's norms and values, it thinks about how we ought to behave according to society.

13) During the __________ stage children gain a sense of control over the environment as their mothers try to toilet train them.

14) __________ is a result of getting either too much or too little pleasure during a psychosexual stage.

15) __________ is a psychoanalytic defense that involves banishing anxiety-arousing thoughts, feelings, and memories right out of consciousness.

16) __________ is a psychoanalytic defense by which people disguise their own threatening impulses by attributing them to others.

17) __________ is a psychoanalytic defense that shifts unacceptable sexual or aggressive impulses toward a more acceptable or less threatening object or person.

18) According to Maslow, the ultimate psychological need that arises after basic physical and psychological needs are met and self-esteem is achieved is called __________.

19) According to Rogers, an attitude of total acceptance towards another person is called __________.

20) The perception that chance or outside forces beyond one's personal control determine one's fate is called __________.

21) __________ disorders are psychological disorders that physically affect the body.

22) A flight from one's home and identity along with amnesia is called a __________ state.

23) People with __________ are continually tense and apprehensive, and they are usually in a state of autonomic nervous system arousal.

24) Depressed feelings may come from __________,

the feeling that you can't do anything to alleviate your pain or make your life better.

25) A person with __________ alternates between the hopelessness and stagnation of depression and the overexcited state of mania.

26) A __________ person has an exaggerated sense of his own importance, and he expects to be catered to and admired by all.

27) __________ is a severe disorder that splits people from reality and is characterized by hallucinations and delusions.

Guide to Dining in Appleton, Wisconsin.

Victoria's: *College Avenue. Fine Italian food with enormous portions. Don't believe any stories the locals tell you. It doesn't get any better than this.*

Sammy's Pizza: *Oneida Street. Thin crust pizza the way it was meant to be served. Atmosphere is comfortable and the service is friendly and familiar.*

Dos Banditos: *Between the Locks, South River St., in "the Flats." The Mexican food is piquant and plentiful. This location is also the only place to purchase one of the area's finest beers: Adler Brau.*

Christie's: *In the Paper Valley Hotel, College Avenue. Christie's is a five-star, nationally recognized restaurant. Some of the best food available anywhere. Take out a loan before you go.*

Friar Tuck's: *College Avenue. This is a local chain. The waitresses (and waiters, if there are any) are required to wear silly and revealing costumes (some of us like this, some don't). Despite this, prices are dirt cheap for traditional American sandwiches and fried food.*

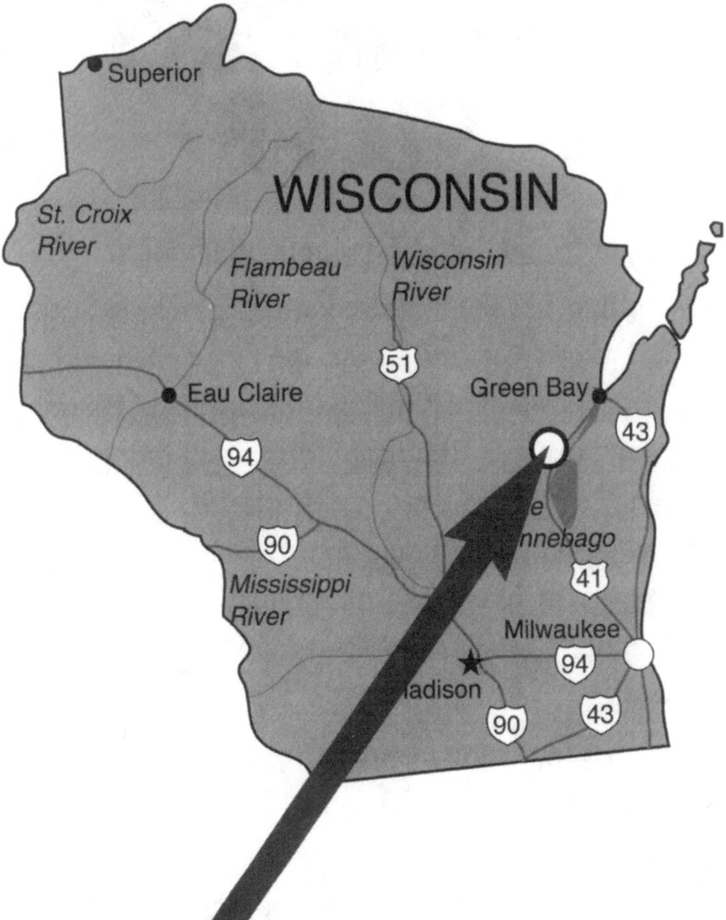

WISCONSIN

Superior

St. Croix River

Flambeau River

Wisconsin River

51

Eau Claire

Green Bay

43

94

90

Mississippi River

41

Milwaukee

94

90

43

Appleton, WI

"Czecho-slovakia? That's like going to Wisconsin. You're in, you're out, no one will ever know."

"Yeah, well I got my ass kicked in Wisconsin once."

-Bill Murray and Harold Ramis, *Stripes*

OTHER IMPORTANT STUFF

STUFF.1: **Psychological Schools of Thought**

OK, here are the main schools of psychological thought we've covered so far: biological, behavioral, cognitive, psychoanalytic, and humanistic. There is one other school of thought worth mentioning even though it's really old and really specific, and that's because it's almost always on the test. It's called **ethology**, which is the study of animal behavior. The main thing to know is Lorenz's classic study of **imprinting**.

Imprinting is the instinct of newly hatched ducks and geese to follow and become attached to the first moving thing they see and hear. Lorenz arranged for himself to be the first thing a group of newly hatched ducks saw. Indeed, the baby ducks followed him rather than their mother. (There is a great picture of this in every Psych 1 textbook.)

STUFF.2: Research Methods

You remember learning about the nature-nurture debate. Well, **twin studies** and **adoption** studies are two effective ways of determining whether a variable is genetically (nature) or environmentally (nurture) determined. If we study identical twins brought up in different environments and find out that they both became schizophrenic, we can assume genetic factors played a crucial role. That's a good example of a twin study.

Adoption studies are used similarly in that they study whether children are more like their biological parents or more like their adoptive parents. Overall, using both twin studies and adoption studies, it has been found that nature *and* nurture interact with one another in determining rates of disorders, personality development, likes and dislikes, and just about everything else.

There's also a fifth research design that we didn't mention: *quasi-experimental*. In the quasi-experimental research design, the researcher still makes observations and can make hypotheses about the causation of events in the experiment. But unlike experimental studies, the researcher does not manipulate the independent variables.

"My cat's breath smells like cat food."
-Ralph Wiggum, *The Simpsons*

STUFF.3: Analysis of Research

Analysis of research refers to the process of organizing and describing data through the use of statistics. The researchers first gather the data, of course, but they also use statistics to describe and analyze the data, as well. The most important descriptions of the data show which numbers (or scores) are most common in the data, or what the average of all the data is. Three ways to do this are to look at:

the **mode**--the most frequently occurring score

the **mean**--the average of the scores

the **median**--literally the middle point, or middle score

All of the data for the experiment is usually in the form of a long list of scores. The scores usually have values distributed according to a **bell curve** or **normal distribution**, which means that most scores fall near the mean and fewer and fewer near the extremes. Just knowing how to describe the data

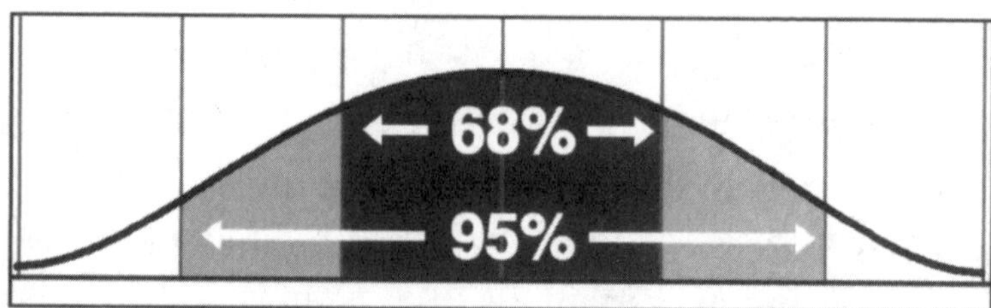

isn't good enough. The researchers must also statistically prove that the data they have isn't a result of random chance.

Statistical tests are used to determine if the difference in the means of two sample groups is **statistically significant**, meaning that the differences between the groups did not occur by chance.

S.A.T.

For example, if you were interested in finding out whether SAT scores are a good predictor of college GPAs, you could study whether there is a statistically significant difference in college GPAs between students in group A, who had high SAT scores, and students in group B, who had low SAT scores.

The statistical tests used to determine significance can become quite complex, but the logic behind them is always the same: the **sample** being tested should be an *accurate representation* of the **population** being hypothesized about, and the averages of the samples should be **reliable** measures. Reliable measures are based on many observations of a large sample with little variability.

STUFF.4: Neurons and the Nervous System

In the video you learned all about the central ner-

vous system and the peripheral nervous system. There is another system, the **endocrine system**, which you should also know a little bit about. The endocrine system is responsible for secreting **hormones** that travel through the bloodstream.

Two important glands in the endocrine system are the adrenal gland and the pituitary gland. In dangerous situations, the **adrenal gland** releases *epinephrine* and *norepinephrine* (adrenaline and noradrenaline), which increase heart rate, blood pressure, blood sugar, and energy level. The **pituitary gland** releases hormones that influence growth and sex drive.

The **brain** is what controls the activity of both the nervous and the endocrine systems. The brain allows the mind to work. It decides what and how the mind should see, hear, think, remember, feel, speak, dream, and so on. Unfortunately, the brain is made up of a lot of boring parts with a lot of hard to remember names, BUT

quite often a handful of these terms will wind up on your test so you'll want to know them, AND besides, you'll sound smart walking around knowing what an amygdala is. Okay, here goes.

The brain "begins" at the **brainstem**, which connects the spinal cord to the skull and which swells at its end forming the **medulla**. The medulla controls heartbeat and breathing. Inside the brainstem is the **reticular formation**, which plays an important role in controlling arousal.

On top of the brainstem is the **thalamus**, which serves as a "switchboard," receiving and sending neural messages. Behind the brainstem is the **cerebellum**, which controls voluntary movement.

Cerebellum company photo

Study Sidekick

The **limbic system** sits between the brainstem and the cerebral hemispheres. It is associated with fearful and aggressive emotions and basic drives like hunger and sex. As part of the limbic system, the **amygdala** is associated with aggression, the **hippocampus** with memory, and the **hypothalamus** with intense pleasure and metabolic rates.

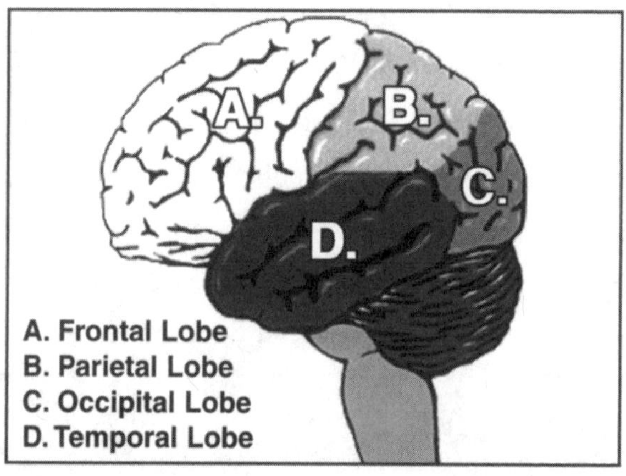

The cerebral hemispheres are the body's ultimate control and information-processing centers and are covered by the **cerebral cortex**. The hemispheres are divided into four lobes: the **frontal lobe**, which is involved in speaking and muscle movements and in making plans and judgments; the **parietal lobe**, which includes the sensory cortex; the **occipital lobe**, which is involved with vision; and the **temporal**

lobe, which is involved with hearing. At the rear of the frontal lobe lies the **motor cortex**, which controls movement; at the front of the parietal lobe is the **sensory cortex**, which registers and processes body sensations.

The rest of the cortex is involved with interpreting, integrating, and acting on information brought to it. These **association areas** are involved in the higher mental functions: learning, remembering, thinking, and speaking. **Broca's area** directs the muscle movements involved in speech, and **Wernicke's area** is involved in language comprehension. Damage to either of these areas results in **aphasia** (impairment of language).

The **corpus callosum** connects the left and right hemispheres of the brain. The **right hemisphere** is involved with visual perception and recognition of emotion, while the **left hemisphere** is involved with verbal skills. Information from the left half of one's field of vision is received only by the right hemisphere, and information from the right half of one's field of vision is received only by the left hemisphere. Normally, the information is then transmitted across the corpus callosum so that the whole brain may process all incoming information.

People who have *split-brain* damage (severed corpus callosum) cannot communicate information taken in from the left side of the brain to the right side of the brain, and vice versa. This can result in some pretty bizarre events. For example, a person may read a visual message which is sent to her right hemisphere, then act on it, but not be able to verbalize that she has taken action or have any idea why she did.

STUFF.5: Sensation

You remember what a **just noticeable difference (jnd)** is--the smallest difference a person can detect between two stimuli. Here's some new information: the jnd will increase as the magnitude of the stimulus increases.

For example, if a you add an ounce of water to two ounces of water, you'll notice; if you add an ounce of water to 10 ounces of water, you probably won't notice. Remember, if you can't tell the difference, that means you're under the jnd. The jnd increases as the magnitude of the stimulus increases.

This concept has been expanded to understanding motivation in humans. For example, a person

earning a $100 will notice a $100 raise, while a person earning $100,000 probably will not.

You learned a lot about eyes and ears in the video, but here's some information on vision and hearing. There are two physical characteristics of light and sound that determine what is seen or heard: **wavelength** and **intensity**. The **wavelength**, which is the distance from one peak of a light wave to the next, determines the *hue* (color) that is seen. With light waves, the shorter the wavelength, the higher the *frequency*, and the bluer the color. With sound waves, the shorter the wavelength, the higher the frequency, and the higher the pitch. The longer the wavelength, the lower the frequency, and the redder the color (or the lower the pitch of a sound). The **intensity**, which is the amount of energy in a light or sound wave, is represented by the wave's *amplitude* (height), which determines the brightness of a color or the loudness of a sound. The greater the amplitude, the brighter the color or the louder the sound. Conversely, the smaller the amplitude of the wave, the duller the color or the softer the sound.

Humans have a few other senses worth touching on, like **touch** (har, har), which occurs through the sensations of *pressure, temperature,* and *pain.*

The sensation of **taste** occurs through *taste buds.* Of all the taste buds on your tongue, each can only taste one of four qualities about what you're eating or drinking: salty, sour, bitter, or sweet. All other tastes are a combination of these four qualities.

Lastly, the sensation of **smell** occurs through *olfactory* receptor cells in your nose.

There are two more senses that almost everyone forgets. **Kinesthesis** is your sense of body position and movement. That's how you know your arm is there, moving to pick up a frothy beverage.

Your sense of **equilibrium** is what keeps you from being dizzy. Equilibrium communicates your body's relation to gravity.

Sensory interaction is the principle that says that one sense may influence another; for example, a food's smell can either enhance or detract from the its taste.

STUFF.6: Perception

Perception is the process of organizing and interpreting sensory information, giving us recognition of objects and events.

Gestalt psychologists study how sensations become perceptions, particularly how humans tend to integrate pieces into wholes. That's what gestalt means in German: a whole, singular, monolithic thing.

Gestalt psychologists suggest that first we create **figure-ground** perceptions, organizing visual stimuli into objects (figures) and background; then we organize stimuli into coherent groups, a process that is called (surprise) **grouping**.

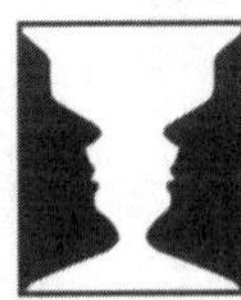

Figure-ground: vase or faces?

They have identified five ways in which we group stimuli together:

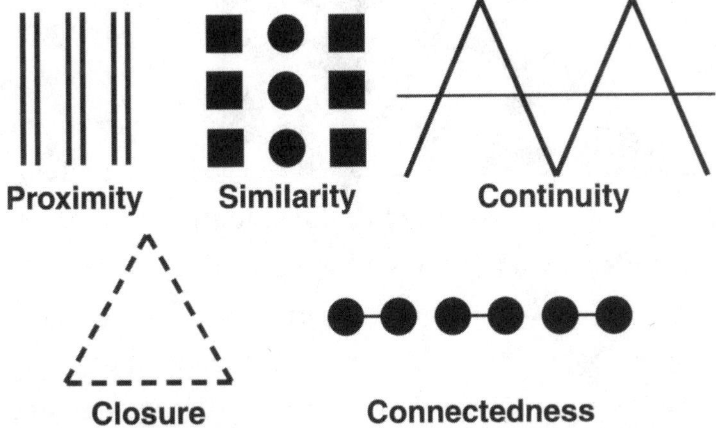

(1) through **proximity**--the perceptual tendency to group nearby figures together;

(2) through **similarity**--the tendency to group similar elements together;

(3) through **continuity**--the tendency to perceive continuous rather than disjointed patterns;

(4) through **closure**--the tendency to fill in gaps; and

(5) through **connectedness**--the tendency to see things as units.

The existence of **depth perception**, the ability to see objects in three dimensions, has been dramatically studied in infants through the use of the **visual cliff**. In this experiment, a flat piece of glass is placed over the edge of a tabletop and is securely fastened to the table. Babies are then placed on the table; to the babies, it looks like they could fall off the edge of the table, even though they really can't. Even infants who are being coaxed by their mother's voice will not crawl over the perceived "cliff".

STUFF.7: Motivation

There are a lot of theories of **motivation** (a need or desire that energizes or directs behavior), but we'll just focus on the one most commonly taught: the **conflict model**.

The **conflict model** of motivation suggests that the choices people make are related to how much energy is required to make them. When a choice is especially difficult to make, the person is in **conflict**: a situation involving incompatible or competing goals, needs, demands, or opportunities. There are four common conflict situations:

(1)In the **approach-approach** case the person is equally attracted to two mutually exclusive goals--eating a piece of cake and losing weight.

(2)In the **avoidance-avoidance** case the person is trying to decide between the lesser of two evils--how some people feel when they vote for a presidential candidate.

(3)In the **approach-avoidance** situation a single goal has both positive and negative aspects--taking a vacation is great fun but costs money and takes you away from the office.

(4)The **double approach-avoidance** case puts the

person in the position of having to choose between two or more goals, both of which have positive and negative consequences, like going to a party or studying. Going to the party would be fun and sociable, but tiring and time-consuming; studying would be helpful for your test on Monday, but you've been working hard all semester and you feel you deserve a break. Each option has pluses and minuses.

STUFF.8: Learning

You remember learning all about operant conditioning and reinforcement. Well, there's some more fun stuff to learn about reinforcement. Reinforcements can be given either every time the behavior occurs (**continuous reinforcement**) or only sometimes after the behavior occurs (**partial reinforcement**).

Although partial reinforcement increases the acquisition period because it will take longer to learn the association, it decreases the rate of extinction because the subject will keep "hoping" that the next time the behavior occurs the reinforcement will come.

There are four schedules of partial reinforcement:

Other Stuff

(1) **Fixed-ratio** reinforcement occurs after a specific, unchanging number of responses, like "price per job.

(2)**Variable-ratio** reinforcement occurs after an unpredictable number of responses, like slot machines.

(3)**Fixed-interval** reinforcement is the first response after a specified time, resulting in increased responses as reward time approaches. Say your mail is delivered every day around 2:00. You won't even think about checking your mail in the morning, but at around 1:30 or so you'll check to see if it's there yet, and then again at 1:45, and then again at 1:50, then again at 1:55, 1:58, and 2:00, till it finally shows up.

(4)**Variable-interval** reinforcement involves a response at unpredictable time intervals. This is why you do your homework every night, even though your professor doesn't collect it every single day--in the fear that you may get to class, only to have the professor ask for your homework.

Some evidence suggests that animals engage in cognitive processes beyond simple stimulus-response (behavior-reinforcement) pairings. For example, one can observe the process of **latent learning** in rats

who have been exposed to a maze without a reward, as compared to rats who have not been exposed to the maze.

When a reward is offered for completing the maze, the rats which have run the maze before run it faster, suggesting they have created a **cognitive map** of the maze, or that they have learned it without external reward.

Another type of learning we discussed earlier is **modeling**. Modeling is most likely to occur in subjects when the action being modeled is consistent with verbal instructions from the model. If a parent wants a child to be a reader, for example, he should read in front of the child and tell the child positive things about reading (vs. do as I say, not as I do).

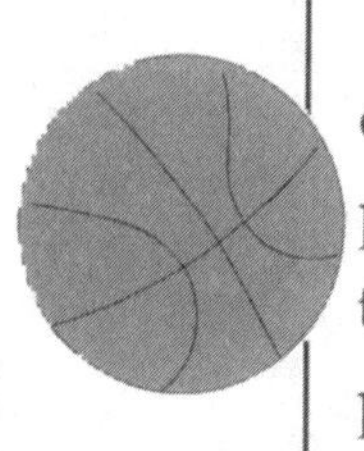

Also, individuals are most likely to model their own behavior after people they admire and respect, people they see as similar to themselves, and people they perceive as successful. That's why ad campaigns use basketball stars to encourage school attendance. Modeled behaviors that are rewarded are more likely to recur than modeled behaviors that are punished (like when a smoker punishes his child who, for some strange reason, has also picked up the habit).

STUFF.9: Memory and Forgetting

You remember the three stages of information processing: encoding, storing, and retrieval. Here is some more stuff to remember. (You know, we have to stop here and let you know we realize how funny that previous paragraph is. We're working on *Memory and Forgetting,* and now we're going to have you *remember* more stuff about it. It really was all unintentional.)

The **Ebbinghaus retention curve** suggests that the amount a person learns depends on the amount of time spent learning. In other words, the more time you spend learning the more you will retain. The **spacing effect** suggests that more information is retained when rehearsal is distributed over time rather than through mass study (in other words, cramming is barely better than nothing--barely). The **serial position effect** suggests that people tend to recall the first and last items on a list.

The sensory memory is the first place information goes to be processed. It is made up of the **iconic memory** and the **echoic memory**.

Iconic memory (a photographic memory lasting no more than a few tenths of a second) was discov-

ered by Sperling. He flashed a group of nine letters (three rows and three columns) in front of subjects for 1/20th of a second. Subjects could not recall all nine, but if asked to remember any one of the rows or columns they could. This suggests that for an instant the eyes register the whole field, but that they can only retain it for a fraction of a second. This is evidenced by the fact that subjects were able to recall any three of the nine numbers flashed in front of them, but when asked to name the fourth, however, they didn't have a clue.

Echoic memory is a momentary sensory memory of auditory stimuli which explains the phenomenon of "hearing" what someone said just as you're saying, "What?"

Long-term memories are made up of **explicit memories** [memories of facts and experiences that one is consciously aware of (the whats)] and implicit memories [memories of skills, preferences, that kind of thing, that one is not consciously aware of (the hows)].

There are two different types of retrieval. **Recall** involves retrieving information previously learned, like you do on a fill in the blank test. **Recognition** involves identifying information previously learned,

like a multiple choice test. Re-learning tests have shown that it takes less time to learn a list of words previously learned but forgotten. This suggests that we *remember* more than we can *recall*.

Priming is the use of associations to a particular memory to "jog" the memory of something else, like remembering the name of a TV show by recalling which actors were in it. Research has shown that memory recall is best when tested under similar contexts, suggesting it is best to learn coursework in the classroom, if that is where you'll be tested.

When trying to remember past events, we often reconstruct things not exactly as they occurred. Elizabeth Loftus's classic studies illustrate the **misinformation effect**: after witnessing an event but then receiving misleading information about that event, subjects will incorporate the new, misleading information into their "memory" of the event.

"I laughed, I cried, I ate a whole tub of mayonnaise!"
-The King

In one instance, Loftus surveyed people who had witnessed a car accident. The witnesses who were asked how fast the cars were traveling right before they "smashed" into each other "remembered" them to be traveling much faster than witnesses who were asked how fast the cars were traveling before they "hit" one another.

STUDY SIDEKICK

Cognition is everything associated with processing, understanding, and communicating information. We can assess people's cognitive abilities through the use of cognitive tests such as the **Wechsler Adult Intelligence Scale (WAIS)**, which specifically assesses **intelligence**--the capacity for goal-directed and adaptive behavior, including the ability to profit from experience, solve problems, reason, and successfully meet challenges and achieve goals.

WAIS

The WAIS is made up of various sub-tests that rate verbal and performance abilities like vocabulary, comprehension, memory, mathematics, problem solving, social judgment, et cetera. Level of intelligence appears to be highly influenced by hereditary factors, although environmental conditions clearly play a role as well.

"Hip isn't about having rhythm; hip is about being happy with who you is." -Igor

The goal of assessment techniques is to distinguish individuals based on ability, so they clearly should not distinguish individuals based on cultural background. Some have suggested, however, that some of the WAIS questions are more likely to be familiar to white, middle-class Americans than to members of other cultural groups. If this is so, then the WAIS may not accurately reflect intelligence.

STUFF.10: Development

Human development progresses through **critical periods**, which are early developmental periods during which particular events are essential. A popular theory in human development is the idea of **stage development**--organizations of behaviors and thoughts that occur in different stages.

A newborn has certain **reflexes** that predispose it to survive. Due to the **rooting** reflex, an infant will open his mouth to search for a nipple when touched on the cheek. **Sucking** and **swallowing** reflexes exist as well. The similar facial expressions of infants of all cultures when they are happy, sad, scared, or surprised suggests that facial expressions are universal and that emotions are basic to human nature.

The development of **morality** is best understood by looking at Kohlberg's stages of morality and his classic study which posed the following dilemma: a man's wife was dying of cancer and he couldn't afford to pay for a drug that would cure her. He tried to borrow the money from everyone he knew but he could only gather half the amount. He asked the pharmacist to accept partial payment with a promise that he would pay the other half as soon as he could. The pharmacist refused, declaring, "I dis-

covered the drug and I want to make money from it." The man got desperate, broke into the drug store and stole the medication to cure his wife.

Kohlberg then asked whether what the man did was right or wrong, and why. As a result of his research he outlined three stages of moral development:

1) **Pre-conventional** ideas of morality (before age nine) revolve around the threat of punishment or the possibility of reward. Typical responses include, "If you let your wife die, you will get in trouble," or, "If you save your wife, you'll be a hero."

2) **Conventional** ideas of morality (by early adolescence) may revolve around conventional wisdom--upholding laws because they are laws. On the other hand, other conventional ideas of morality revolve around the idea of gaining social approval. Typical responses include, "If you steal the drug, everyone will think you are a criminal."

3) **Post-conventional** ideas of morality (ideally develop after adolescence) follow basic ethical principles. Typical responses include, "People have a right to live," or, "If you steal the drug, you won't have lived up to your own ideals."

Other Stuff

Adolescence is a particularly trying period of development and involves traversing from childhood to adulthood, from dependence to independence. Adolescence entails three primary things: **puberty** (sexual maturation); developing a stable **identity** (sense of self) by testing and integrating various roles; and an ability to be **intimate** (to form close and loving relationships).

The ultimate end of development is, of course, death. Kubler-Ross observed that people facing death go through five stages:

1)**Denial**: A patient resists the idea that he is dying; he refuses to believe it.

2)**Anger**: The patient stops denying that he is dying and becomes angry at people who are in good health, angry at medical professionals, angry at God or anyone else who happens to be around.

3)**Bargaining**: The patient tries to come up with ways to postpone death: "I will be very religious if I am allowed to live to see my granddaughter get married."

4)**Depression**: The patient starts to realize the futility of bargaining and becomes depressed. He experiences "preparatory guilt" for his own death.

(5)**Acceptance**: The patient mourns the loss of his life and accepts his impending death. He often becomes unemotional, seeming at peace and ready to die.

Keep in mind that most people teach these stages, but the stages are by no means concrete. Many people don't experience all the stages, and not everyone experiences them in the same order.

STUFF.11: **Personality Development**

People who have been faced with repeated traumatic events, or people who put too much emphasis on external factors, resign themselves to never being able to avoid aversive events. This resignation is called **learned helplessness** and has been studied in depth by Seligman.

Seligman conducted the classic study in which dogs were initially given an electric shock that they were able to escape by jumping over a hurdle. The dogs were then repeatedly shocked without the opportunity to escape. Finally, the dogs were again allowed to escape the shock by jumping over a hurdle. Instead of choosing to escape, however, the poor pups simply whimpered helplessly in a corner. The

dogs had learned to be helpless.

Personality can be assessed through the use of various assessment techniques such as the **Minnesota Multiphasic Personality Inventory (MMPI)**, which primarily assesses personality disorders by asking subjects to respond to hundreds of true/false statements like, "No one seems to understand me," "I get angry often," and "Sometimes voices tell me to do things." The MMPI is scored by comparing the subject's answers to norms compiled by a computer. The results may reveal if the subject is having somatic difficulties, is depressed, has work troubles, relationship problems, or a psychological disorder.

On the other hand, projective techniques for assessing personality are scored *subjectively,* (according to the interpretation of the person scoring the test). The **Rorschach** test is a series of ambiguous inkblots that are presented to a subject. The subject is then asked what the blots might be. The responses are interpreted as indicative of how the subject sees and interprets ambiguous stimuli in his or her day to day life.

The **Thematic Apperception Test (TAT)** is a series of pictures depicting people engaging in neutral

interactions. The pictures are presented to a subject, who then tells a story about what might be happening. The stories are used to hypothesize about important people, themes, and conflicts in the subject's life.

STUFF.12: **Social Theory and Development**

"The postman only knocks twice, so if you hear four knocks, you know it's just some wise-guy trying to pawn off his junk mail on you."
-Igor

Attitudes are beliefs or feelings that induce someone to respond in a particular way to particular objects, people, and events. When our attitudes about something are not consistent with our actions, we experience **cognitive dissonance**--a discomfort resulting from the inconsistency of our thoughts and behaviors. As a result, we often change our attitudes to fit our actions.

Here's a quick example of cognitive dissonance: many students come to college wanting to study hard and make good grades (who doesn't?) but then feel uncomfortable with their desires to go out and party, leaving studying by the wayside. The discomfort caused by the clash between studying and partying is called cognitive dissonance.

Conformity was extensively studied by Solomon Asch. Asch's classic study asked college students to

indicate which of four lines was the same length as a standard line. The students were unknowingly in the presence of three confederates (people who pretend to be subjects but are really working with the experimenter).

The experiment went like this: the first few times, the confederates would go first and would all pick what was obviously the right line. The student would then pick the obviously correct line, as well. Then, on say the fourth trial, all three confederates picked what was clearly the wrong line. What would inevitably happen is that the college student would think for a while and then pick the same wrong line that the other three had picked.

An even more dramatic study, focusing on **obedience**, was conducted by Stanley Milgram. Milgram told pairs of subjects that he was studying the affects of punishment on learning, when he was actually studying obedience. He told a pair of subjects participating in the experiment that one subject would be randomly selected to be the "teacher" and one subject would be randomly selected to be the "student."

In actuality, however, a confederate was always playing the role of the "student." The experimenter then told the "teacher" that he had to teach the "stu-

dent" word pairs. If the student was incorrect, the teacher would have to shock the student. The voltage would increase with each successive incorrect response.

Milgram found that, despite visible signs of pain (and even screaming), 63% of the "teachers" continued to administer high levels of shock. The teachers continued just because they were told to do so by the experimenter. These studies have been used to illustrate how something as incomprehensible as the obedience of Nazi soldiers to torture and kill could occur. (Incidentally, like Watson's experiment on Little Albert, experiments like Milgram's are no longer allowed today. Don't be afraid to participate in psychological studies.)

Altruism is helping others without regard for one's self-interests. When will we help others? Amazingly enough, we are *less* likely to help others when there are *more* people around us, a phenomenon known as the **bystander effect**. This is because we are less likely to notice the incident, less likely to interpret it as an emergency, and less likely to assume responsibility. However, if a positive model is helping, and we are not in a hurry, we are more likely to help. Positive mood and feelings of guilt enhance the likelihood that

we will assume responsibility.

STUFF.13: Abnormal Psychology

The **medical model** of psychology maintains that, since diseases have physical causes that can be diagnosed, treated, and (in most cases) cured, psychological disorders should be similar. The medical model assumes that psychological illnesses can be diagnosed based on their symptoms and then cured through therapy. Disorders are diagnosed according to the **Diagnostic and Statistical Manual of Mental Disorders (DSM-IV).** Systematically classifying disorders is useful for describing, treating, and researching disorders. The use of labels, however, focuses attention on the similarities between disorders, rather than on how each person is uniquely experiencing and expressing distress.

STUFF.14: Treatment and Therapy

Bio-medical therapy treats psychological disorders by altering the way the brain functions. This can be done through the use of drugs, which alter the electrochemical transmissions of the brain. *Antipsychotic drugs* such as *chlorpromazine* are similar

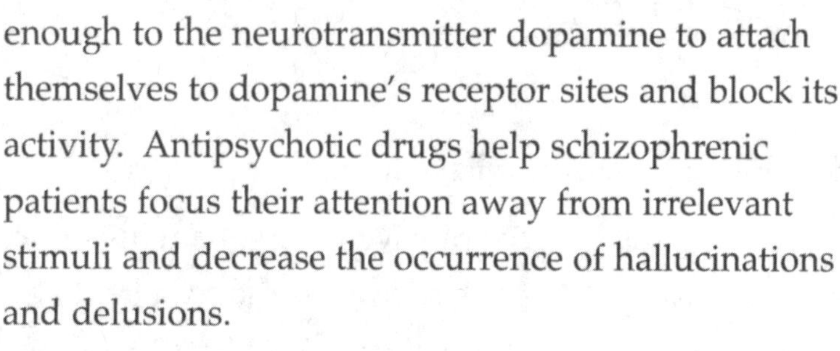

enough to the neurotransmitter dopamine to attach themselves to dopamine's receptor sites and block its activity. Antipsychotic drugs help schizophrenic patients focus their attention away from irrelevant stimuli and decrease the occurrence of hallucinations and delusions.

Antianxiety drugs such as *valium* depress central nervous system activity and, therefore, create a calmer internal state. *Antidepressant drugs* increase the availability of the neurotransmitters norepinephrine and serotonin, which elevate arousal and mood.

Although drugs are widely used to treat the symptoms of many disorders, they often have unwanted side effects, fail to address the underlying causes of the disorder, and are most effective when used in conjunction with psychotherapy.

Psychotherapy is an emotional, confidential interaction between a psychotherapist and a person suffering from a psychological difficulty. Different psychotherapeutic techniques include:

1)**Psychoanalysis**: Through the process of free association (saying anything that comes to mind), the analyst and patient attempt to find the unconscious root of seemingly illogical patterns of thought and

behavior. Inevitably, the flow of free association will halt due to a feeling that the mind is blank or a feeling that a thought that has come to mind is embarrassing, unacceptable, inappropriate, irrelevant, etc.

Any censoring of thoughts is considered to be **resistance**, which involves blocking anxiety-laden material from consciousness. The means of resistance (the way the patient has chosen to defend against the emergence of anxiety-provoking material) is **interpreted** by the analyst.

The analyst uses phrases such as, "It seems like you're feeling embarrassed to talk about sexual relations," in order to make the patient aware that he or she is "resisting," and in order to discover underlying wishes, fears, or conflicts that have been repressed.

This process is assisted by the phenomenon of **transference**--the transference of feelings for important people in one's life (past and present) onto the analyst and then interpreting those transferred feelings as feelings for the analyst.

In other words, a patient may resist her analyst because she has feelings for her analyst which she interprets as genuine, when, in actuality, her true feelings have just been *transferred* to the analyst. The ulti-

mate goal of psychoanalysis is to help the patient gain *insight* into his or her conflicts and effect change through increased understanding and self-awareness.

2)**Humanistic therapy** also emphasizes that increased self-awareness brings about change. In contrast to psychoanalytic therapy, humanistic therapy only focuses on becoming aware of *present* feelings and *conscious* thoughts. The technique used in humanistic therapy is **person-centered therapy**.

In **person-centered therapy**, the therapist engages in **active listening**--genuine, accepting, and empathic listening to whatever the client says without interrupting or offering interpretations. The therapist reflects (repeats back) what the client is saying in order to show how actively he or she is listening. The ultimate goal is to provide a safe environment where the natural tendency towards healthy personal growth can flourish.

3)**Behavioral therapy** uses learning principles to eliminate unwanted behaviors. Behaviorists do not believe that searching for unconscious determinants or becoming more self-aware are the keys to changing behavior. Behaviorists focus on, well, behavior. Their goal is to eliminate unwanted and problematic behaviors by use of **counter-conditioning**.

Two **counterconditioning** techniques used are **systematic desensitization** and **aversive conditioning**. **Systematic desensitization** is often used to treat phobias. Systematic desensitization involves associating a state of relaxation with a situation that provokes anxiety. The idea is, you can't feel anxious and relaxed at the same time. If, while a person is in the presence of an anxiety-provoking stimulus, he uses relaxation techniques (deep breathing, muscle relaxation), the anxiety will be eliminated.

Aversive conditioning is a process which associates an unpleasant state with an unwanted behavior. That means that whenever you do something you're not supposed to do, something really bad happens. An example would be causing nausea in an alcoholic patient whenever the patient is drinking alcohol.

Token economies are a another form of **operant conditioning** that involve reinforcing desired behaviors and withholding reinforcement of undesirable behaviors. Subjects earn tokens for exhibiting desired behaviors or not exhibiting undesirable behaviors. The tokens can then be cashed in for various privileges or treats. Such behavior modification techniques work best with children and inpatients. However, long-term change is rare--as soon as the

reinforcement system is removed, the unwanted behaviors return.

4)**Cognitive therapy** attempts to address the criticisms of behavior therapy by widening the focus from just the problem behavior. Cognitive therapy attempts to alter the thought processes that precede the behaviors. If a person were depressed, for example, the cognitive therapist would use various techniques to try to change his thought patterns from self-defeating to self-helping.

One technique is **rational-emotive therapy**, in which the therapist vigorously confronts and challenges a person's illogical, self-defeating attitudes and assumptions.

Another technique, **cognitive behavior theory**, tries to make a person aware of his or her irrational negative thinking and replace it with new ways of thinking and talking. The patient practices these new ways of thinking and talking in everyday situations. The therapist would pick apart the faulty logic in statements such as, "If I fail this test I will never get into college, everyone will hate me, and I'll be a failure." The therapist would teach the patient to restructure his or her thought processes and make more positive self-statements such as, "This is a diffi-

"We're all in the gutters, but some of us are looking at the stars."
-The Pretenders

cult test but, I studied hard for it and I'll do the best I can; where I go to college depends on more than just this test score."

5)**Group therapies** administer one of the above therapies (except psychoanalysis) to small groups of patients. The group setting allows the patients to learn from each other in a supportive environment. Often, a patient's condition can improve greatly just through the knowledge that others experience the same problems.

Family therapy treats the family as a system in which each individual member contributes to the desirable and undesirable behaviors of the other members. The ultimate goal of family therapy is to increase communication between family members.

How I Came to be a Writer

an autobiographical fable

Igor

Years ago, in the sleepy college town of Madison, Wisconsin, my mom and dad got together to go to the hospital. At that time, hospitals were exciting and served free food to newlyweds and people who were ill. My parents had gotten married for just such an occasion. They got to the

hospital at about 8 PM on December the ninth. My dad ordered chicken, and my mom ordered salmon. Dad got the chicken, but Mom ended up with me instead. She tried to return me, insisting that I had no gills, and that I certainly wasn't going to be tasty with dill. The hospital stuck to their guns, however, and I became a member of the family.

As I grew up, my mom was always supportive. She taught me to catch and throw baseballs. She made sure I knew how to read street signs. And most importantly, she taught me that most bus lines go in both directions.

My dad was just as helpful as my mother. He's an artist. Through my dad, I was always learning about art--how to hold a canvas, how to wash brushes, and which paintings to spit on in galleries.

So I guess it makes sense that when I finished high school, there were tons

of colleges trying to recruit me. After a few months, I had narrowed down my choices to two: The Pewaukee School of Zen Haircare, and The College of Lazy Sycophants in Urbana, Illinois. Unfortunately, both institutions burned down on January 19, 1990, so I went to The George Washington University in Washington, DC.

At GW **everything is happy**. I really enjoyed my time there. If there was anything I didn't like, **it was nothing at all.** While in Washington, I learned to play hockey. The game stayed my main hobby until I graduated with a degree in journalism, with a minor in psychology.

Things were looking good. I had been drafted by the Flames, and played a few games for the Calgary Hitmen. After three preseason games, I had 5 goals and 3 assists. During my fourth game, I went to dig for the puck along the boards in the right corner. I

never even noticed the check coming. I was blind-sided by a 300-pound defenseman who broke nearly 50% of the bones in my body. It hurt a little. Physical therapy was okay, and the doctors were nice enough to give me the gills I asked for.

I was too disabled to ever play hockey again. I needed to find another profession. I wanted something that would allow me to sit in front of a computer all day, eat cheese-steaks, and drink lots of coffee. There weren't any openings at NASA, so my only choice was to become a writer.

I've been writing for a while now. Sometimes, when I'm frustrated, I check my boss into the water cooler. Being a writer is pretty fun.

PSYCHO STRESS RELIEF

PsychoSearcho

Solution: 91 Letters

```
I N H G E G O C E N T R I C N
E E A A O E N T T V I N H E O
G R L E C N E G I L L E T N I
E O L A L G A P E N E I B O S
M P U E D P N P R S R R S I S
A S C F L E A I E U A S N S E
L V I S U A L C L I F F I S R
S O N R N D U U N E G T N E G
Y M A R O R G S S S D O X R E
N O T R D I T E B I R O E P R
A I I C A E V C C U O N M E H
P D O A M D T A E I N N E R T
S A N A D A S N H I C P S L I
E L S A G E P W K E R L U J O
Y F I V E B L S C E B O E N E
```

BRAIN STEM
DELUSIONS
MODELING
REGRESSION
CHEESE CURD
EGOCENTRIC
HALLUCINATIONS
NEURONS
VISUAL CLIFF
BEHAVIORISM
SYNAPSE
FUDGECICLE
INTELLIGENCE
REPRESSION
SKINNER
SPAM

Psycho Stress Relief

PsychoCrosso

ACROSS

2 Readying info for transmission
4 Focuser
8 State of being stuck
9 Traffic directors
11 Recycling receptacle
12 Go fast
15 American status symbol
17 Not yours
18 Sucky cousin of FM
19 Way to ___
20 Friend of to
21 Sitting place
22 Bottom of your thinker
24 Stop
25 Bright thing in the sky
26 Big weight
29 Conveyer of conversation
34 Self-actualizer
35 Where it's ___
36 Salmon for bagels
38 Friend of fro
39 Id's enemy
42 Chart
44 Long, skinny neuron part
45 Obsessive-Compulsive Disorder
46 How to figure out number stuff
47 States of forgetting stuff and splitting

DOWN

1 Rat learning chamber
3 The group you don't mess with
5 Theory tester
6 The hierarchy guy
7 The newest book of psych disorders
9 Being like everybody
10 The little tree guys on nerve cells
13 The company that made this book
14 Teenagers have raging ________
16 Spiced ham
21 Grouping for better memory
23 Picking up a behavior
27 Frozen pudding on a stick
28 Losing ability to speak
30 ________ of grandeur
31 Feeling
32 World's largest exporter of cranberries
33 Cognitive construction
37 Leap
40 Guilt and desire mediator
41 Pleasure seeker
43 Thing connected to shoulder

GLOSSARY

absolute threshold - The smallest stimulation needed to detect a specific stimulus.

accommodation - In cognitive theory, the reworking of a framework of beliefs to fit new information or experiences.

acquisition - The first stage of learning, during which a response is established and gradually strengthened. In classical conditioning, the time period during which a stimulus starts to evoke a conditioned response. In operant conditioning, the augmentation of a reinforced response.

action potential - A neural impulse, a short electrical charge that travels down an axon.

active listening - In Rogers' person-centered therapy, empathic listening in which the listener echoes, restates, and clarifies.

adrenal glands - Two glands just above the kidneys,

part of the endocrine system. The adrenal glands secrete the hormones epinephrine (adrenaline) and norepinephrine (noradrenaline), which help arouse the body in stressful situations.

altruism - Helping others without regard for one's self-interests

amnesia - Loss of memory.

amygdala - Two neural centers in the limbic system that are related to emotion.

anal stage - The second of Freud's psychosexual stages, from about 18 months to 3 years, when bowel control is learned and pleasure is centered on bowel and bladder control.

anxiety disorder - Psychological disorders characterized by excessive anxiety or maladaptive behaviors to reduce that anxiety. Includes phobias and obsessive-compulsive disorders.

antisocial personality disorder - A personality disorder in which the person exhibits a lack of conscience

for wrongdoing, showing no remorse for harming others, even friends and family members.

aphasia - Impairment of language because of brain damage

arousal theory - A theory of motivation that claims that some behaviors come from our desire to increase arousal instead of reduce arousal.

assimilation - In cognitive theory, the fitting in of new information and experiences into an already existing framework.

association areas - Areas of the brain not involved in primary motor or sensory functions; they are involved in higher mental functions.

associative learning - Learning that certain events happen concurrently. The events can be two stimuli (in classical conditioning) or a response and its consequences (operant conditioning).

attachment - A close emotional bond with another person; young children seek closeness to their care-

giver and show distress on separation. Adults seek attachment in emotional support of friends of family.

attitude - A belief and feeling that predisposes a person to respond in a specific ways to stimuli.

attribution theory - The theory that humans are inclined to give a causal explanation for the behavior of others, often explaining the behavior to either the situation or the person's disposition.

automatic processing - Thinking or comprehension which requires no conscious effort.

aversive conditioning - A form of counter-conditioning that associates an unwanted behavior (such as drinking alcohol) with unpleasant state (like Jersey. No, we're just kidding. Like painful, debilitating stomach cramps).

axon - The extension of a neuron which ends in branching terminal fibers. Messages are sent through axons to other neurons or to muscles or glands.

basic trust - Erik Erikson's idea of a notion that the everything is predictable and trustworthy; basic trust is thought to be formed during infancy by suitable experiences with responsive caregivers.

behavior therapy - Application of learning principles and Behaviorist theory to the elimination of unwanted behaviors.

behaviorism - The view that psychology should be an objective science that only studies observable behavior.

biological psychology - A branch of psychology which focuses on the link between biology and behavior.

bipolar disorder - A mood disorder in which a person varies between depression and mania.

blind spot - The point at where the optic nerve leaves the eye, where no receptor cells are located.

brainstem - The central core of the brain, near where the spinal cord swells as it enters the skull; it is

responsible for survival functions.

Broca's area - The area of the left frontal lobe that directs the muscle movements involved in speech.

Bystander effect - The tendency of an individual to not help others in need if there are a large number of people around.

Cannon-Bard theory - The theory that emotion-causing stimuli simultaneously trigger physiological responses and the subjective experience of emotion.

central nervous system - The brain and spinal cord.

cerebellum - **1.** The "little brain" attached to the brainstem; it helps coordinate voluntary movement and balance. **2.** One hell of a company

cerebral cortex - The massive folded tissue of interconnected neural cells that covers the rest of the brain; the cerebral cortex is the central control and information-processing center.

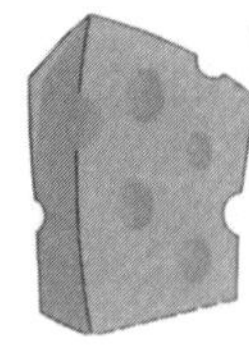

cheese curd - Edible proto-cheese

chunking - Organizing items into manageable clumps; often done automatically.

classical conditioning - A method of learning in which an organism associates events. A neutral stimulus that precedes an unconditioned stimulus (UCS) begins to yield a response that anticipates and readies the organism for the unconditioned stimulus.

closure - The tendency of perception to fill in gaps, allowing perception of disconnected parts as a whole object.

cochlea - A fluid-filled tube in the inner ear. Sound waves through the cochlea trigger nerve impulses which allow perception of sound.

cognitive behavior therapy - A cognitive therapy that attempts to teach patients to alter their own way of thinking to achieve changes in feelings and behavior.

cognitive dissonance theory - The theory that humans act to reduce the discomfort (dissonance) felt

when thoughts (cognitions) are inconsistent.

cognitive map - A mental picture of the layout of one's environment.

cognitive psychology - A branch of psychology which studies thought processes: thinking, knowing, remembering, and communicating information.

cognitive therapy - Therapy that teaches people new, more adaptive ways of thinking and acting; based on the assumption that thoughts intervene between events and our emotional reactions.

conditioned response (CR) - In classical conditioning, the learned response to a stimulus that does not normally elicit a response. (CS).

conditioned stimulus (CS) - In classical conditioning, a neutral stimulus that when associated with an unconditioned stimulus (UCS), triggers a conditioned response.

cones - Retinal receptors that detect color and fine detail.

concrete operational stage - In Piaget's theory, the stage of cognitive development (from about 6 or 7 to 11 years of age) during which children obtain the ability think logically about concrete events.

conformity - Adjustment of behavior and/or thinking to match with a group norm.

connectedness - The tendency of perception to see features as a single unit when they are uniform and linked.

conservation - The principle that properties such as mass, volume, and number are constant despite changes in their form.

continuity - The perceptual tendency to organize stimuli into smooth patterns.

continuous reinforcement - Reinforcing a response whenever it occurs.

control group - In experiments, the control groups is the portion of the random sample that does not receive treatment, so it can be compared to the exper-

imental group.

conversion disorder - A somatoform disorder in which yields genuine physical symptoms for which no physiological basis can be found.

corpus callosum - The largest bundle of neural fibers that connects and the right and left hemispheres of the brain.

correlational study - A research design which studies the relationship between two variables and how much factors vary together.

counterconditioning - A behavior therapy in classical conditioning that conditions new responses to stimuli that already trigger unwanted behaviors.

critical periods - Times shortly after birth when an organism's development is most susceptible to exposure to certain influences in the environment.

defense mechanisms - In psychoanalytic theory, the ego's means of reducing stress by unconsciously distorting reality.

delusions - False beliefs about self or environment that sometimes accompany schizophrenia.

dendrites - The branching parts of a neuron that receive and conduct impulses toward the cell body.

dependent variable - In an experiment, the factor that is being measured; ideally, the dependent variable changes in response to manipulations of the independent variable.

depth perception - The ability to perceive objects in three dimensions even though images that strike the retina have only two-dimensions; allows judgment of distance.

descriptive study - A research design involving systematic observation and description of behavior.

DSM-IV - The American Psychiatric Association's Diagnostic Statistical Manual of Mental Disorders (Fourth Edition), the most widely accepted system for classifying psychological disorders.

difference threshold - The smallest difference that a

someone can detect between two stimuli. Also called the just noticeable difference (jnd).

displacement - A psychoanalytic defense that shifts stress-causing sexual or aggressive impulses toward a more acceptable or less threatening object or person.

discrimination - In classical conditioning, the ability to distinguish between a conditioned stimulus and a different, unrelated stimulus that has similarities to the CS. In operant conditioning, responding differently to different stimuli.

dispositional attribution - Explaining other people's behavior by their internal characteristics.

dissociative disorders - Psychological disorders in which the individual loses awareness some part of consciousness memories, thoughts, or feelings.

"Real tomato ketchup, Eddie?"
Clark Griswald

drive-reduction theory - A motivation theory that asserts that discomfort associated with physiological needs creates an aroused psychological state. That arousal drives the person to reduce the need.

echoic memory - A brief sensory memory of auditory stimuli (three or four seconds)

effortful processing - Encoding which needs attention and conscious effort.

ego - In psychoanalytic theory, the conscious part of personality that mediates the demands of the id, superego, and reality.

egocentric - In Piaget's theory, the inability of the preoperational child to take another's point of view.

emotion - A response of the whole organism, involving physiological arousal, expressive behavior, and conscious as well as unconscious experience.

encoding - The processing of information by linking it to to concepts already learned. Allow information to be sent into the memory system.

endocrine system - The body's set of glands which secrete hormones into the bloodstream.

experimental group - The group in an experiment

that is exposed to the treatment, and then compared to the control group.

experimental study - A research design in which the researcher manipulates one or more factors (independent variables) to determine what effect, if any, they have on some behavior or mental process (the dependent variable).

explicit memories - Memory of facts and experiences.

external locus of control - The perception that chance or outside forces decide one' fate.

extinction - Decreased occurrence of a response in classical conditioning, when an unconditioned stimulus (UCS) does not follow a conditioned stimulus (CS); operant conditioning, when a response is no longer reinforced.

family therapy - Psychological treatment of the family as a system. Considers an individual's unwanted behavior to be influenced by or directed at other

family members; attempts to have family members foster positive relationships and improved communication.

feature detectors - Nerve cells in the brain that respond to particular parts of a stimulus, like movement, positioning or shape.

figure-ground - The organization of the visual field into objects (the figures) that differ from their surroundings (the ground).

five-minute major - Major hockey penalty. Applied to penalties which are committed with intent to injure.

fixation - In psychoanalytic theory, a lingering focus of pleasure-seeking energies at an earlier psychosexual stage, where conflicts were unresolved.

fixed-interval schedule - In operant conditioning, a schedule of reinforcement that reinforces a certain amount of time after the first response.

fixed ratio schedule - In operant conditioning, a rein-

forcement schedule that reinforces after a specific number of responses.

frequency - The number wavelengths per period of time.

frontal lobe - The section of the cerebral cortex just behind the forehead; controls speech and muscle movements, and is involved in making plans and judgments.

fudgecicle - Frozen chocolate pudding on a stick.

fugue states - A dissociative disorder, amnesia accompanied by flight from home.

fundamental attribution error - The observer's tendency to underestimate the impact of the situation and environment, and to overestimate the impact of personal disposition in the assessment of behavior..

generalization - When stimuli similar to the conditioned stimulus to evoke similar responses.

generalized anxiety disorder - An anxiety disorder

which creates a continuous state of autonomic nervous system arousal, the sufferer is tense, and apprehensive.

genital stage - The last psychosexual stage, which begins in puberty; the sexuality matures and pleasure is sought through sexual contact.

grouping - Organizing stimuli into coherent chunks.

hallucinations - Sensory experiences which have no basis in reality.

hierarchies - Organizing information into categories and further organizing into subcategories.

hierarchy of needs - Maslow's pyramid-like scale of human needs, beginning at the bottom with physiological needs, higher up are safety needs and then psychological. Each need must be satisfied before moving on to the next higher level.

hippocampus - A neural center in the limbic system that processes explicit memories for storage.

hormones - Chemicals messengers, manufactured by

the endocrine glands. Hormones are produced in one tissue and affect other tissues.

Hoss - Dog of all dogs. Real brains behind Cerebellum Corporation and the Standard Deviants. Able to hold six golf balls in mouth at one time. Doesn't like snausages.

humanistic psychology - A branch of psychology concerned with the strivings of healthy people for self-realization.

hypothalamus - A neural structure below the thalamus that helps to govern the endocrine system with the pituitary gland. The hypothalamus is also linked to emotion.

iconic memory - A picture-image memory that lasts no more than a few tenths of a second.

id - In psychoanalytic theory, an unconscious portion of self that strives for instantaneous satisfaction of basic sexual and aggressive drives.

identity - Sense of self; according to Erikson, the

"To crush your enemies, to see them driven before you and to hear the lamentations of deir women."
-Conan the Barbarian

adolescents seek to firm up a sense of self by testing and integrating different roles.

imagery - Mental pictures; a most helpful in effortful processing.

implicit memories - Non-descriptive recollection (skills, preferences, and dispositions).

imprinting - A process in which certain young animals form attachments very early in their life.

incentive theory - A theory of motivation which studies the factors that lure us into an aroused state.

independent variable - In an experimental design, the variable that is manipulated

in-group - The social group to which one belongs.

in-group bias - The tendency of individuals to favor their own group.

intelligence - The ability to acquire and utilize knowledge.

intensity - The amount of energy in a light or sound wave, as determined by the wave's amplitude.

internal locus of control - An individual's perception of self-control of fate.

interpretation - In psychoanalysis, the analyst's attempts to elucidate the patient's resistances and other significant behaviors in order to promote patient insight.

interviews - A research method which asks subjects to describe themselves.

intimacy - The ability to form close, loving bond with another person; in Erikson's theory, a primary task in early adulthood.

iris - The colored portion of the eye around the pupil that controls the size of the pupil opening.

James-Lange theory - The theory that emotion results from awareness physiological responses to stimuli.

just-world hypothesis - People's propensity to believe the world is just and therefore others get what they deserve and deserve what they get.

latency stage - The fourth psychosexual stage, from about age 6 to puberty, in which sexual impulses are repressed.

latent learning - Learning that is not apparent until there an incentive is available.

learned helplessness - Hopeless resignation learned when no escape is offered to avoid repeated aversive events.

lens - The transparent structure in the eye that focuses images onto the retina.

limbic system - A set neural structures at the edge of the brainstem; associated with fear and aggression and drives like food and sex.

long-term memory - The storehouse of the memory system, which has an indefinitely large capacity.

major depressive disorder - A mood disorder in which a person, for no discernable reason, experiences two or more weeks of feelings of despair, worthlessness, and/or diminished interest or pleasure in most activities.

mean - The arithmetic average of a distribution.

median - The middle score in a distribution, so that half the scores are above it and half below it.

medical model - The psychological application of the assumptions of medical care. Diseases have physical causes that can be diagnosed, treated, and, in most cases, cured. Therefore, "mental" illnesses can be diagnosed on the basis of their symptoms and cured through therapy.

medulla - Base of the brainstem which controls heartbeat and breathing.

middle ear - The chamber between the eardrum and the cochlea which contains three tiny bones, (hammer, anvil, and stirrup) which concentrate the vibrations of the eardrum on the cochlea.

Minnesota Multiphasic Personality Inventory (MMPI) - The most popular personality test. Very extensive, (550 questions) the MMPI was originally designed to assess psychological disorders.

misinformation effect - Witnesses tend to change their interpretation of an event when they receive misleading information about it afterwards.

mode - The most frequently occurring score in a distribution.

modeling - Learning a behavior through observation and imitation of others.

mood disorders - Psychological disorders characterized by extreme emotion.

motor cortex - A section of the brain near the rear of the frontal lobes that controls voluntary movement.

multiple personality disorder - A dissociative disorder which a patient exhibits two or more personalities in the same body. The personalities may or may not be aware of the others' existence.

myelin sheath - An insulating layer of fatty cells encasing the fibers of many neurons; allows faster transmission of neural impulses.

narcissistic personality disorder - A personality disorder characterized by an exaggerated sense of self-importance, and an expectation of esteem from others.

nature-nurture issue - The long-standing controversy over whether biology or environment have a greater effect on thought and behavior.

negative reinforcement - In operant conditioning, the removal of unpleasant or aversive stimuli to increase the likelihood of a response.

neuron - A nerve cell; the basic building block of the nervous system.

neurotransmitters - The chemical messengers that link the synaptic gap between neurons.

normal distribution - A distribution of scores which yields the greatest proportion of returns in the mid-

dle range, and substantially fewer at the extremes. Normal distributions usually form symmetrical, bell-shaped curves. Most psychological tests return normal distributions.

observation - A research method in which detailed descriptions of the subject are made.

obsessive compulsive disorder - An anxiety disorder characterized by repetitive, unwanted thoughts (obsessions) and/or ritualistic actions (compulsions).

occipital lobe - The part of the cerebral cortex lying at the back of the head; visual areas are centered in the occipital lobe.

operant conditioning - Learning in which behavior is strengthened by reinforcement.

object permanence - The comprehension that things continue to exist even when not seen.

oedipus complex - According to Freud, a boy's sexual desires toward his mother and feelings of jealousy and hatred for the rival father. According to

some psychoanalysts, a parallel Electra complex occurs in girls.

optic nerve - The nerve that carries neural impulses from the eye to the brain.

oral stage - The first of Freud's psychosexual stages, which lasts from birth to about 18 months, during which pleasure centers on the mouth.

outer ear - Part of the ear that funnels sound waves to the eardrum.

out-group - A discernable social group to which you do not belong.

parallel processing - A kind of problem solving in which several aspects of a problem are processed simultaneously.

paranoid personality disorder - A personality disorder characterized by hostility, excessive suspicion, guardedness, and an inability to trust others.

parietal lobe - The section of the cerebral cortex near

at the top of the head; includes the sensory cortex.

partial reinforcement - Reinforcing a response only at random times; yields slower acquisition of a response but a much greater resistance to extinction than does continuous reinforcement.

perception - Processing of sensory information, enabling recognition of meaningful objects and events.

peripheral nervous system - The nerve cells that connect the central nervous system to the rest of the body. It consists of sensory neurons which carry messages from the body's sense receptors, and the motor neurons, which carry messages to the muscles and glands.

person-centered therapy - A humanistic therapy developed by Carl Rogers. The therapist uses active listening within a genuine, accepting, empathic environment to help facilitate clients' growth.

personal control - Sense of control over environment.

personality disorders -Psychological disorders characterized by maladaptive behavior patterns.

phallic stage - The third of Freud's psychosexual stages, from about ages 3 to 6, during in which sexual feelings arise toward the parent of the other sex, and the pleasure zone is centered in the genitals.

phobic disorders - Anxiety disorders marked by persistent, irrational fears of a specific situation or objects.

pitch - A tone's highness or lowness, which depends on frequency.

pituitary gland - The endocrine system's primary gland. The pituitary gland regulates growth and controls the activities of other endocrine glands.

pleasure principle - The id demands immediate gratification of its base needs.

positive reinforcement - In operant conditioning, a reward that will increase the likelihood of a behavioral response.

preoperational stage - In Piaget's theory, the stage (from about 2 to 6 or 7 years of age) when a child learns to use language but cannot perform mental operations of concrete logic.

primary reinforcer - An innately reinforcing stimulus.

priming - The activation, often unconscious, of particular memory associations.

proactive interference - The effect of prior learning which disrupts the recall of new information.

projection - A defense mechanism to disguise threatening impulses by attributing them to others.

proximity - The perceptual tendency to group events that occur near each other.

psychoanalysis - Freud's technique of treating psychological disorders based on his theories of psychosexual development. The patient's free associations, resistances, dreams, and defense mechanisms -and the therapist's interpretations of them - allegedly

allow the patient to gain self-insight.

psychoanalytic psychology - A branch of psychology concerned with how unconscious motivations affect thought and behavior.

psychological disorder - A condition exhibiting behavior which is judged to be atypical, disturbing, maladaptive, and unjustifiable.

psychology - The scientific study of behavior and mental processes.

psychosexual stages - In psychoanalytic theory, the stages of development during childhood during which the id focuses pleasure-seeking energies on distinct erogenous zones.

psychotherapy - A deeply personal and emotional interaction between a trained therapist and a patient, aimed at alleviating psychological difficulty.

punishment - An uncomfortable event that is intended to decrease the behavior it follows.

pupil - The adjustable opening in the center of the eye through which light enters.

random assignment - Assigning subjects to experimental and control groups by chance, so that each individual has the some chance of being selected for a particular group. This minimizes the effect of preexisting differences between those assigned to the different groups.

rational-emotive therapy - A confrontational form of cognitive therapy developed by Albert Ellis, that challenges people's illogical, self-defeating though processes.

rationalization - A psychoanalytic defense mechanism that offers self-justifying explanations in place of the real, more threatening, conscious or unconscious for behavior.

reaction formation - A psychoanalytic defense mechanism in which the ego unconsciously switches unacceptable thoughts, feelings, or actions into their opposites.

reality principle - In psychoanalysis, the ego's usually satisfies the id's desires in ways that are realistic and acceptable.

recall - A variety of memory that allows a person to retrieve information learned earlier, like a fill-in-the-blank test.

recognition - A variety of memory which allows a person to identify items previously learned, as like a multiple-choice test.

regression - A psychoanalytic defense mechanism that involves reverting to a more immature psychosexual stage where some psychic energy has remained fixated.

rehearsal - The deliberate repetition of information, either to keep the information in consciousness or to encode it for storage.

relearning - A memory scheme that judges the amount of time necessary when re-acquiring previously learned information.

replication - Repetition of a the concepts of a research study, but in a different field or situation, to see whether the basic finding generalizes to other subjects and other circumstances.

repression - A psychoanalytic defense mechanism that banishes anxiety-arousing thoughts, feelings, and memories from consciousness.

research designs - Varieties of experiments. See experimental, correlations, and descriptive.

research methods - How psychologists gather information. See tests, interview, and observations.

resistance - In psychoanalysis, the blocking anxiety-laden material from consciousness.

reticular formation - An area in the brainstem that is important in controlling arousal.

retina - The inner surface of the eye, which contains light sensitive rods and cones, and layers of neurons that begin the processing of the visual information.

retrieval - Getting information out of storage in the memory.

retroactive interference - When new learning disrupts the recall of old information.

rods - Neurons that detect black, white and gray.

rooting reflex - A baby's instinct to open the mouth and search for a nipple when the baby is touched on the cheek.

Rorschach Inkblot Test - The popular projective test. Ten inkblots, used to help to identify people's inner feelings by analyzing their interpretations of the blots.

scapegoating - Blaming a group other than your own for your misfortunes or hardships. No casual link exists for blame, the out-group is simply convenient or available.

Schacter's two factor theory - The theory that to experience emotion a physical response must occur, and the individual has to be able to recognize and

label that response.

schema - A piece of mental framework that organizes and interprets information.

schizophrenia - A psychotic disorder characterized by disorganized and deluded thinking, disturbed perceptions, and inappropriate emotions and actions.

scientific method - Method used by psychologists to study psychological phenomena. See theory and hypothesis.

secondary reinforcer - A conditioned reinforcer that gains its power by its association with the primary reinforcer.

self-actualization - Maslow's ultimate psychological need; the complete fulfillment one's potential, which only occurs after all other needs have been met.

self-serving bias - A willingness to perceive oneself favorably.

sensation - The process by which sense receptors and

the nervous system receive stimuli from the environment.

sensorimotor stage - In Piaget's theory, the stage (from birth to about 2 years) during which infants perceive the world in terms of their sense and motion

sensory cortex - The area of the brain at the front of the parietal lobes that detects and processes body sensations.

sensory interaction - The idea that senses can influence each other.

sensory memory - Initial, immediate recording of sensory information by the memory system.

serial position effect - Our ability to best recall the last and first items in a list.

shaping - In operant conditioning, a practice in which reinforcers guide behavior toward a desired goal.

short-term memory - Memory that holds a few items

for a short period of time before they are stored or forgotten.

similarity - The perceptual tendency to group elements that are alike.

situational attribution - The attribution of behavior to external characteristics.

Skinner box - A chamber containing a bar or key that an animal can manipulate to obtain a food reinforcer, attached to the bar or key are devices to record the animal's rate of bar pressing or key pecking. Used in operant conditioning research.

social facilitation - Improved performance on tasks when the task is performed in the presence of others; happens with simple or well-learned tasks; tasks that are difficult or not yet mastered are usually flubbed when performed in the presence of others.

social loafing - The tendency for people in a group to exert less effort when the group members are pooling their efforts toward attaining a common goal. Loafing does not occur when group members

are individually accountable.

Somatoform disorder - Psychological disorders in which the symptoms take a physical form without apparent physical cause.

spacing effect - Distributed study or practice (lots of short trials instead of one long one) to yield better long-term retention than through massed study or practice.

spontaneous recovery - The reappearance of an old conditioned response (without provocation).

Standard Deviants - Sycophantic masochists who like to learn difficult subjects and teach them to others. Ultimately responsible for the destruction of Pompeii.

storage - The retention of encoded information over time.

stranger anxiety - The fear of strangers that infants commonly display starting at about eight months of age.

sublimation - A psychoanalytic defense mechanism by which patients re-channel their unacceptable impulses into socially acceptable activities.

surligor - Condition that occurs when an editor is pestered and annoyed. Surligor is grumpy and combative. Most co-workers avoid surligor, if possible.

synapse - The space between the axon of one neuron and the dendrite or cell body another neuron.

systematic desensitization - A type of counter-conditioning that associates a pleasant state with anxiety-triggering stimuli. Commonly used to treat phobias.

temporal lobe - The part of the cerebral cortex on the sides, lying roughly above the ears; includes the auditory areas.

tests - A research method which measures how a subject responds to a particular events or problems.

thalamus - The brain's sensory routing area, located on top of the brainstem; it directs messages from the body and brainstem to the sensory receiving areas in

the cortex, and transmits replies from the brain to the cerebellum and medulla.

Thematic Apperception Test - A projective test in which people allegedly express their inner feelings and interests through the stories they create to explain ambiguous scenes which are presented to them.

token economy - An operant conditioning procedure with a delayed, variable rewards schedule. Desired behavior earns the patient tokens. A patient exchanges a token of some sort, earned for exhibiting the desired behavior, for various privileges or treats.

transference - In psychoanalysis, the patient's attribution of emotions linked with other relationships to the therapist.

unconditional positive regard - A device for client-centered therapy; an attitude of total acceptance toward the client.

unconditioned response (UCR) - In classical conditioning, the unlearned, naturally occurring response

to a unconditioned stimulus (UCS)

unconditioned stimulus (UCS) - In classical conditioning, a stimulus that naturally triggers a response.

unconscious - Impulses, thought, or feelings that an individual has, but is not aware of.

variable-interval schedule - In operant conditioning, a schedule of reinforcement that reinforces a response at intervals that vary around a mean, but the subject cannot predict.

variable-ratio schedule - In operant conditioning, a schedule of reinforcement that reinforces a response after a certain number of responses, the number of which varies around a mean, and is not predictable by the subject.

Vezina Trophy - Award given to the NHL's outstanding regular-season goaltender. The winner in for 1995-1996 was Jim Carey of the Washington Capitals.

visual cliff - A laboratory apparatus designed to test depth perception in infants and young animals.

VIDEO NOTES

wavelength - The distance from the peak of one light or sound wave to the peak of the next.

Wechsler Adult Intelligence Scale (WAIS) - The most widely used intelligence test; contains verbal and performance (nonverbal) subtests. The most recent version is the WAIS-R.

Wernicke's area - An area of the left temporal lobe of the brain which is involved in language comprehension.

"The sun, with all those planets revolving around it and dependent on it, can still ripen a bunch of grapes as if it had nothing else in the universe to do."
-Galileo

PRACTICE TEST

1) Psychologists who believe that both heredity and environment contribute to personality development believe in the __________ approach to understanding human behavior.

a) nature
b) nurture
c) nature-nurture
d) natural selection

2) The four steps in the scientific method are utilized in what order?

a) hypothesis - theory - study - refinement
b) theory - hypothesis - study - refinement
c) study - theory - hypothesis - refinement
d) study - hypothesis - theory - refinement

3) Which of the following are examples of research methods?

a) tests, interviews, and correlations
b) tests, classical conditioning, and scapegoating
c) interviews, observations, and negative reinforcement
d) tests, interviews, and observations

4) The experimental factor that an investigator

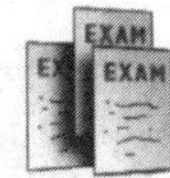

manipulates is called the __________.

a) independent variable
b) dependent variable
c) effective variable
d) control variable

5) __________ is used to assure that different results between two experimental groups is not due to differences in the subjects.

a) validity
b) reliability
c) random assignment
d) replicability

6) __________ are used to clearly describe the exact procedures used in an experiment.

a) descriptive studies
b) dependent variables
c) observations
d) operational definitions

7) __________ carry neural messages from the central nervous system to the muscles.

a) sensory neurons
b) interneurons
c) motor neurons
d) moron neurons

8) Which part of the neuron receives the neural messages coming in from other neurons?

a) the dendrites
b) the cell body
c) the axon
d) the neurotransmitters

9) The __________ is a layer of fatty cells that insulates the axon which helps to speed the travel of impulses.

a) acetylcholine
b) myelin sheath
c) dopamine
d) motor cortex

10) The space between neurons is called the __________.

a) axon
b) association areas
c) synapse
d) iris

11) The __________ of a stimulus is the smallest amount of a stimulus that you can detect.

a) difference potential
b) just noticeable difference
c) action potential
d) absolute threshold

12) The point where the optic nerve leaves the eye is called the __________.

a) rod
b) cone
c) pupil
d) blind spot

13) The __________ theory best explains why people eat when they are hungry, drink when they are thirsty, etc.

a) instinct
b) drive-reduction
c) arousal
d) incentive

14) The __________ theory best explains why you might feel hungry after smelling food cooking even though you weren't hungry before that.

a) instinct
b) drive-reduction
c) arousal
d) incentive

15) According to __________, to experience emotion, you have to have a physical response to a stimulus and you have to be able to recognize and label that response.

a) the Cannon-Bard theory

b) the James-Lange theory
c) Schacter's two factor theory
d) Maslow's hierarchy of needs

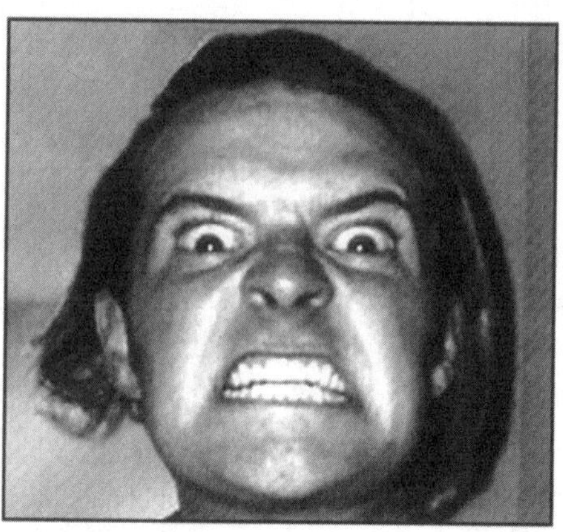

Mr. Steam's employees did not always work up to their potential, and Mr. Steam did not like that. When Mr. Steam didn't like something, he would blow up. This scared his employees and caused them to cry. Right before Mr. Steam would blow up at his employees for being incompetent fools, his face would turn red and his eyes would bulge. Soon, his employees would cry at the sight of Mr. Steam's red face and bulging eyes.

16) Mr. Steam blowing up is the __________.

a) unconditioned stimulus
b) conditioned stimulus
c) unconditioned response

d) conditioned response

17) Mr. Steam's red face and bulging eyes are the __________.

a) unconditioned stimuli
b) conditioned stimuli
c) unconditioned responses
d) conditioned responses

18) The employees crying because Mr. Steam blew up is the __________.

a) unconditioned stimulus
b) conditioned stimulus
c) unconditioned response
d) conditioned response

19) The employees crying because Mr. Steam's face turned red and his eyes started to bulge is the __________.

a) unconditioned stimulus
b) conditioned stimulus
c) unconditioned response
d) conditioned response

20) If the employees started to cry when Mr. Steam's face turned purple this would be an example of __________.

a) acquisition
b) generalization
c) discrimination
d) extinction

21) John Steam Jr.'s face turns red, his eyes bulge, and he blows up, when other children don't share their toys with him. This is an example of __________.

a) classical conditioning
b) operant conditioning
c) modeling
d) shaping

Mrs. Okra told her children that if they ate all of their brussels sprouts, pureed peas, and cooked carrots, they could have a slice of chocolate covered chocolate ice cream cake with chocolate chips and chocolate cookies with chocolate milk.

22) After her children ate only the brussels sprouts, Mrs. Okra gave them their chocolate delight. This is an example of __________.

a) acquisition
b) discrimination
c) shaping

d) spontaneous recovery

23) The chocolate delight is an example of __________.

a) positive reinforcement
b) negative reinforcement
c) punishment
d) instant tooth decay

24) If Mrs. Okra told her children that if they ate their brussels sprouts, pureed peas, and cooked carrots that they would never have to clean up their toys or make their beds, she would be using __________.

a) positive reinforcement
b) negative reinforcement
c) punishment
d) Dr. Spook's advice

25) Mrs. Okra told her children that if they didn't eat their brussels sprouts, pureed peas, and cooked carrots, she would force them to watch Barney all day. Watching Barney all day is an example of __________.

a) positive reinforcement
b) negative reinforcement
c) punishment
d) torture

26) Every morning Dana Dolittle would eat 2 ounces of Colonel Crunch cereal with 3/4 cup of skim milk, drink 8 ounces of orange juice and 2 cups of coffee. While grocery shopping, Dana Dolittle was shocked to discover that Colonel Crunch also comes peanut butter flavored. Dana decided to alter his schema for what constitutes a morning meal and he added the peanut butter flavored Colonel Crunch to his breakfast repertoire. This is an example of _________.

a) attachment
b) development
c) assimilation
d) accommodation

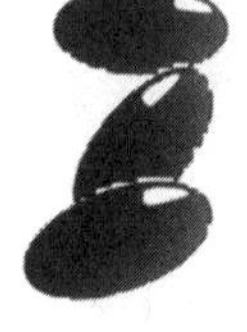

27) Stingy Louie owns a candy store. And, as you might have guessed, he's rather stingy. In fact, he's a cheap liar. He displays two jars of jellybeans for the same price, one is a very tall, thin jar that holds 50 jellybeans and the other is a small, fat jar that holds 100 jellybeans. A lot of the children who come to store point to the tall jar and say "Me want that big jar of jellybeans." Louie gets away with this because these children do not understand the concept of _________.

a) assimilation
b) accommodation
c) object permanence

d) conservation

28) A few years later, one of these children comes into the candy store and dumps a tall, fat jar of marshmallow fluff onto Louie's head and says, "That's for screwing me out of 46,700 jellybeans." This child has entered __________.

a) the sensorimotor stage
b) the preoperational stage
c) the concrete operational stage
d) stage left

29) When a child can distinguish loved ones from strangers, he may develop __________.

a) stranger anxiety
b) object permanence
c) conservation
d) a schema

30) Harry Harlow's study of baby monkeys' reactions to two artificial monkey mothers made out of wire [one with a bottle sticking out of it, and one wrapped in a soft terry cloth] was an attempt to show that __________ is a basic human need.

a) attachment
b) object permanence
c) accommodation

d) scapegoating

31) Anne and Tara both get A's on their quantum physics final. Anne says, "I'm not surprised that I got an A; I'm so smart it didn't matter that I didn't get any sleep the night before. But I just can't believe Tara got an A; she's so stupid it shouldn't matter how hard she studied." Anne fell victim to the __________ in explaining her grade, and she committed the __________ in explaining Tara's grade.

a) self-serving bias and social facilitation
b) scapegoating and the fundamental attribution error
c) social facilitation and the fundamental attribution error
d) self-serving bias and fundamental attribution error

32) On opening night, Ms. Starr performed better than she ever had during rehearsals. Claiming she just loves a great audience, she attributes her success to __________.

a) conformity
b) scapegoating
c) social facilitation
d) social loafing

33-46)On the next page, draw a line from the word on the left to its meaning on the right.

PRACTICE TEST

33) retrieving

34) effortful processing

35) hierarchies

36) encoding

37) storing

38) chunking

39) automatic processing

40) rehearsal

41) imagery

42) proactive interference

43) sensory memory

44) long term memory

45) short term memory

46) retroactive interference

a) getting information into the brain

b) retaining information into the brain

c) getting information back out of the brain

d) effortless encoding, like reading a word you already know

e) encoding that requires effort and conscious processing

f) repeating information to help encode it

g) visualizing information to help encode it

h) organizing information into familiar units in order to encode it

i) a higher level of organizing information in order to encode it, like an outline

j) the first place information goes as it comes in through the senses

k) can only store 7 (+ or - 2) chunks of information

l) limitless and relatively permanent storehouse of information

m) the disruptive effect of prior learning on the recall of new information

n) the disruptive effect of new learning on the recall of old information

47) The __________ theory proposes that unconscious motivations influence personality development.

a) behaviorist
b) psychoanalytic
c) humanistic
d) social-cognitive

48) The __________ theory focuses on what people think, and how their interpretations of what's going on around them affect their responses to environmental stimuli.

a) behaviorist
b) psychoanalytic
c) humanistic
d) social-cognitive

49) The __________ theory focuses on human potential and the drive for self-actualization.

a) behaviorist
b) psychoanalytic
c) humanistic
d) social-cognitive

50) The __________ seeks immediate gratification of sexual and aggressive needs.

a) id

b) ego
c) superego
d) ego ideal

51) The ego tries to meet the needs of the id the best it can according to the __________.

a) pleasure principle
b) reality principle
c) conscience
d) unconscious

52) Children who get most of their pleasure from sucking, biting, and chewing are in the __________ psychosexual stage.

a) oral
b) anal
c) phallic
d) genital

Circle T(true) or F (false) for the following descriptions of defenses.

53) Repression is banishing anxiety-arousing thoughts, feelings, and memories from consciousness. **T / F**

54) Regression is retreating to an earlier stage of

development. T / F

55) Reaction formation is when you take your anger, or some other unacceptable impulse, and divert it from its source to something or someone else. T / F

56) Rationalization is when people disguise their own threatening impulses by pinning them on other people. T / F

57) Sublimation is rechanneling unacceptable impulses into socially acceptable activities. T / F

58) According to Maslow, the ultimate psychological need that arises after basic physical and psychological needs are met and after self-esteem is achieved is called __________.

a) unconditional positive regard
b) genuineness
c) self-actualization
d) humanism

Allison woke up one morning and had no idea where she was or who the people in her house were. She decided to flee her home and take off for California. When Allison's mother, Betsy, realized Allison was missing, she cried and cried for weeks, felt worthless, and did not enjoy participating in any

pleasurable activities. When Allison's father, Carl, realized Allison was missing, he began washing his hands every 10 minutes, checking underneath Allison's bed for her, and imagining all kinds of horrible things that could have happened to her. Meanwhile, during Allison's travels, she ran into Douglas who told her that he was on the move too, he suspected that the FBI had tapped all of his phones and bugged his house, and since he wasn't even able to trust his family, he was constantly in a state of flux. Later that day, Allison ran into Ellen, a young woman who thought she was Princess Leah and couldn't remember where she parked the Starship Enterprise.

"She's got some nice buns!"
-Darth Vader to Gen. Grand Moff Tarkin

59) Allison was suffering from __________.

a) conversion disorder
b) fugue state
c) somatoform disorder
d) schizophrenia

60) Betsy was suffering from __________.

a) bipolar disorder
b) antisocial disorder
c) major depressive disorder
d) mania

61) Carl was suffering from __________.

a) obsessive compulsive disorder
b) generalized anxiety disorder
c) conversion disorder
d) somatoform disorder

62) Douglas was suffering from __________.

a) antisocial disorder
b) narcissistic disorder
c) paranoid disorder
d) schizophrenia

63) Ellen was suffering from a __________.

a) antisocial disorder
b) narcissistic disorder
c) paranoid disorder
d) schizophrenia

64) The instincts of newly hatched ducks and geese to follow and become attached to the first moving thing they see and hear is called __________.

a) instinct
b) imprinting
c) incentive
d) hatching

65) If we study identical twins brought up in different environments and find out that they both

became schizophrenic, we can assume __________.

a) genetic factors played no role
b) genetic factors played some role
c) environmental factors played no role
d) the nature-nurture debate is dead

66) If you were testing a new drug by comparing the mean score of group A (patients who received a placebo) to the mean score of group B (patients who received the new drug) you would hope that the difference between the two mean scores was __________.

a) normally distributed
b) reliable
c) valid
d) statistically significant

67) The __________ releases hormones that influence growth and sex drive.

a) adrenal gland
b) brain
c) pituitary gland
d) parietal lobe

Study Sidekick

68) amygdala	a) controls activity of the nervous and endocrine systems
69) aphasia	b) connects the spinal cord to the skull
70) association areas	c) controls heartbeat and breathing
71) brain	d) plays an important role in controlling arousal
72) brainstem	e) serves as a "switchboard," receiving and sending neural messages
73) Broca's area	f) controls voluntary movement
74) cerebellum	g) part of the limbic system associated with aggression
75) corpus callosum	h) part of the limbic system associated with memory
76) frontal lobe	i) part of the limbic system associated with intense pleasure and metabolic rates
77) hippocampus	j) lobe involved in speaking and muscle movements and in making plans and judgments
78) hypothalamus	k) lobe that includes the sensory cortex
79) medulla	l) lobe that is involved with vision
80) occipital lobe	m) lobe that is involved with hearing
81) parietal lobe	n) directs the muscle movements involved in speech
82) reticular formation	o) part of the cortex involved in higher mental functions like learning, remembering, thinking and speaking
83) temporal lobe	p) involved with language comprehension
84) thalamus	q) damage to Broca's or Wernicke's area
85) Wernicke's area	r) connects the left and right hemispheres of the brain

86) According to the __________, the spinal cord contains a neurological "gate" that blocks or allows pain signals to pass on to the brain.

a) gate-control theory of pain
b) neurological theory
c) behaviorists
d) paingate theory

87) The concept that one sensory system may influence another sensory system, for example, the smell of food may enhance or detract from the taste of it, is called __________.

a) sensory intensity
b) sensory interaction
c) sensory perception
d) sensory gate

88) The "visual cliff" was used to study __________.

a) vision in infants
b) motor skills in infants
c) attachment of infants to their mothers
d) depth perception in infants

89) David can't decide if he should spend Spring Break with his buddies in Cancun or with his girlfriend in Paris; he is facing a(n) __________ conflict.

a) approach-approach
b) avoidance-avoidance
c) approach-avoidance
d) double approach-avoidance

90) Why does partial reinforcement decrease the rate of extinction?

a) because the acquisition period increases
b) because generalization does not occur
c) because discrimination decreases
d) because of the hope that reinforcement will occur the next time

91) Which schedule of partial reinforcement results in stop and go responding?

a) fixed-ratio
b) variable-ratio
c) fixed-interval
d) variable-ratio

92) Scott has been studying faithfully all semester and is confident that he will do better on his finals than Greg, who just started studying days before the final. Scott believes in __________.

a) the spacing effect
b) the serial position effect
c) iconic memory
d) echoic memory

Practice Test

93) Iconic memory, a photographic memory lasting no more than a few tenths of a second was discovered by Sperling when his subjects remembered__________.

a) all nine letters in the experiment
b) only the top row of letters
c) only the left column of letters
d) any one column or row

94) The fact that it takes less time to learn a list of words previously learned but forgotten suggests __________.

a) we retrieve more than we encode
b) we recall more than we can remember
c) we store more than we can remember
d) we remember more than we can recall

95) The fact that after witnessing a car accident people who were asked how fast the cars were traveling right before they "smashed" into each other "remembered" them to be traveling much faster than people who were asked how fast the cars were traveling before they "hit" one another is an example of __________.

a) priming
b) an explicit memory
c) an implicit memory
d) the misinformation effect

96) According to Kohlberg's stages of moral development, a person whose ideas of morality revolve around the threat of punishment or the possibility of reward is in the _________ stage.

a) pre-conventional
b) conventional
c) post-conventional
d) presidential conventional

97) According to Kubler-Ross, people facing death go through five stages in what order?

a) denial - depression - anger - bargaining - acceptance
b) denial - anger - bargaining - depression - acceptance
c) bargaining - depression - anger - denial - acceptance
d) depression - anger - denial - bargaining - acceptance

98) A discomfort resulting from inconsistent thoughts and actions is called _________.

a) cognition
b) cognitive difference
c) the misinformation effect
d) cognitive dissonance

99) Which of the following correctly matches the person to the concept associated with him/her?

a) Asch/conformity; Kitty Genovese/obedience; Seligman/bystander effect

b) Asch/learned helplessness; Seligman/conformity; Milgram/obedience
c) Seligman/learned helplessness; Kitty Genovese/conformity; Asch/obedience
d) Kitty Genovese/bystander effect; Milgram/obedience; Seligman/learned helplessness

100) The __________ consists of asking subjects to look at a series of pictures depicting people engaging in neutral interactions and to tell a story about what might be happening in the picture.

a) Wechsler Adult Intelligence Scale -Revised
b) Minnesota Multiphasic Personality Inventory
c) Thematic Apperception Test
d) Rorschach Inkblot Technique

101) Laura goes to see a psychologist because she is feeling depressed. The psychologist prescribes an antidepressant. The psychologist probably ascribes to the __________.

a) bio-medical model
b) psychoanalytic model
c) humanistic model
d) cognitive model

102) Jimmy goes to see a psychologist because he is having trouble disciplining his children. The psychologist suggests he employ a token econo-

my system with his children that rewards desired behaviors and withholds reward for undesirable behaviors. The psychologist probably ascribes to the _________.

a) psychoanalytic model
b) behaviorist model
c) humanist model
d) family systems model

103) Jimmy went away on business. When he returned, he found that his children had misbehaved for the baby-sitter all week. Jimmy decided to ditch the token economy system, figuring he wouldn't always be around to employ it. He went to see a different psychologist. She suggested that Jimmy speak with his children about their behavior. She told Jimmy to try to identify and replace the thought processes that preceded the kids' recklessness. In other words, she told Jimmy to try to change the thought, "If my sister doesn't share her toys, I'll scream," to "If my sister doesn't share her toys, I'll tell her that it upsets me, that I like playing with her and feel hurt when she hoards her toys." This psychologist probably ascribes to the _________ model.

a) behaviorist
b) cognitive
c) psychoanalytic

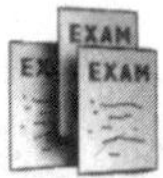

d) family systems

104) Harrison goes to see a psychologist to try to overcome his fear of snakes. The psychologist suggests that if he places himself in the presence of snakes while he's also in the presence of something that relaxes him, his fear of snakes will disappear. This method for treating phobias is called __________.

a) aversive conditioning
b) operant conditioning
c) systematic desensitization
d) rational-emotive

105) Three months after being cured of his fear of snakes, Harrison develops a fear of dogs. He decides to go and see a different psychologist. This psychologist recommends that he begin therapy which will involve exploring the unconscious roots of his fears. This type of therapy is called __________.

a) psychoanalysis
b) rational-emotive
c) family
d) person-centered

106) Harrison soon starts feeling angry at his therapist because he believes she is treating him with the same disrespect that he feels his wife treats

him with. This phenomena is called __________.

a) interpreting
b) resistance
c) active listening
d) transference

107) Harrison becomes frustrated with this intensive therapy and tries another psychologist. This psychologist's ultimate goal is to provide a safe environment where Harrison's natural tendency towards healthy growth can flourish. This psychologist probably ascribes to the __________ model.

a) humanistic
b) psychoanalytic
c) cognitive
d) behavioral

108) Harrison wonders why, no matter what he says, the psychologist is genuine, accepting, and empathic. We know that the psychologist was employing what technique?

a) counterconditioning
b) token economy
c) interpretations
d) active listening

109) It turns out that Harrison is married to Laura and that Jimmy is Laura's ex-husband, so those misbehaving children spend weekends with Harrison and Laura. The children become fed up with the whole situation and go to see a psychologist themselves. This psychologist suggests bringing the whole family in to see if communication between everybody can be improved. This psychologist probably ascribes to the __________ model.

a) cognitive
b) humanistic
c) family systems
d) talk show host

ANSWERS TO QUIZZES AND TESTS

Quiz: PART I

1) behavior and mental processes
2) nurture
3) hypothesis
4) valid
5) laboratory and natural
6) experimental
7) operational definitions
8) random assignment
9) no
10) decreases
11) the brain and the spinal cord
12) neurons, central nervous system, rest of the body

13) receptors, brain

14) brain, receptors

15) dendrites

16) myelin sheath, speeds travel of impulses

17) synapse

18) acetylcholine, dopamine

19) all-or-none firing

20) absolute threshold

21) difference threshold or just noticeable difference

22) accommodation

23) blind spot

24) feature detectors

25) cochlea

26) drive reduction

27) arousal

28) hierarchy of needs

29) self-actualization

30) Schacter's two factor theory or cognitive labeling

Quiz: Part II

1) associative
2) neutral, conditioned
3) acquisition
4) generalization
5) suppressed
6) shaping
7) positive
8) negative
9) punishment
10) modeling
11) chunking
12) short-term memory, fills up
13) retroactive interference
14) cognition
15) assimilation
16) sensorimotor, object permanence, stranger anxiety
17) preoperational, egocentric
18) formal operational

Quiz: Part III

1) attachment
2) basic trust
3) dispositional
4) fundamental attribution error
5) self-serving bias
6) just world phenomena
7) scapegoating
8) social loafing
9) psychoanalytic
10) id, pleasure principle
11) ego, reality principle
12) superego
13) anal
14) fixation
15) repression
16) projection
17) displacement
18) self-actualization

19) unconditional positive regard

20) external locus of control

21) somatoform

22) fugue

23) generalized anxiety disorder

24) learned helplessness

25) bipolar disorder

26) narcissistic

27) schizophrenia

PRACTICE TEST

1) c
2) b
3) d
4) a
5) c
6) d
7) b
8) a
9) b
10) c
11) b
12) d
13) a
14) d
15) c
16) a
17) b
18) c
19) d
20) b
21) c
22) c
23) a
24) b
25) c & d
26) c
27) c
28) c
29) a
30) a
31) d
32) c
33) c
34) e
35) i
36) a
37) b
38) h
39) d
40) f
41) g
42) m
43) j
44) l
45) k
46) n
47) b
48) d
49) c
50) a
51) b
52) a
53) T
54) T
55) F
56) F
57) T
58) c
59) b
60) c
61) a
62) c
63) d
64) b
65) b
66) d
67) c
68) g
69) q
70) o
71) a
72) b
73) n
74) f
75) r
76) j
77) h
78) i
79) c
80) l
81) k
82) d
83) m
84) e
85) p
86) a
87) b
88) d
89) a
90) d
91) c
92) a
93) d
94) d
95) d
96) a
97) b
98) d
99) d
100) c
101) a
102) b
103) b
104) c
105) a
106) d
107) a
108) d
109) c

PSYCHOCROSSO SOLUTION

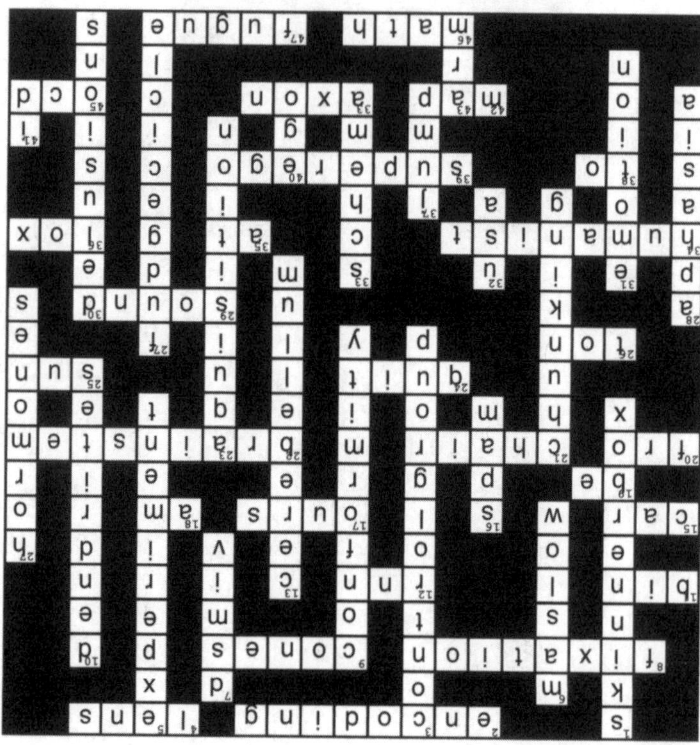

Hey! Hey! Hey!

Once you've found all the words in the PsychoSearcho, there'll be a whole bunch of letters left over. All of those letters are a jumbled up bunch of words. If you can figure out what those words are and what they mean, let us know. We'll send you a bunch of really cool stuff if you get it. Write your answer on a 3x5 card with your name, address, and phone number, and send it to:

PsychoSearcho Jumble
c/o Cerebellum Corporation
1301 Beverly Road, Suite 200
McLean, VA 22101

"Alright. That's it."
-The Man

HANDY DANDY THEORIST CHART

BIOLOGICAL

A branch of psychology concerned with the link between biology and behavior. Bio-medical therapy treats psychological disorders by altering the way the brain functions. This can be done through the use of drugs that alter the electrochemical transmissions of the brain.

BEHAVIORAL — B.F. Skinner

The view that psychology should be an objective science that studies behavior processes without reference to mental processes. Behavioral therapy applies learning principles to the elimination of unwanted behaviors. Counterconditioning and token economies are sometimes used.

COGNITIVE — Jean Piaget

A branch of psychology concerned with all mental activities, including thinking, knowing, remembering, and communicating information. Cognitive therapy teaches people new, more adaptive ways of thinking and acting based on the assumption that thoughts affect our emotional reactions.

HUMANISTIC — Carl Rogers

A branch of psychology concerned with the strivings of healthy people for self-determinism and self-actualization. In Rogers' person-centered therapy, empathic listening is used to help a patient understand himself. Empathic listening has the therapist echo, restate, and clarify what the patient says.

PSYCHOANALYTIC — Sigmund Freud

A variety of psychology based on Freud's theories of psychosexual development. Freud's technique treats psychological disorders by seeking to expose and interpret unconscious tensions. The patient's free associations, resistances, dreams, and transferences (and the therapist's interpretation of them) release previously repressed feelings, allowing the patient to gain self-insight.

Study Sidekick

Personal Notes

STUDY SIDEKICK

PERSONAL NOTES

Study Sidekick

Personal Notes

STUDY SIDEKICK

Personal Notes